Side By Side

Moonshine and Murder in Mississippi

Side By Side

Moonshine and Murder in Mississippi

T. J. Ray

PELICAN PUBLISHING
NEW ORLEANS

Copyright © 2016
By T. J. Ray
All rights reserved

First printing, 2016
Second printing, 2025

> The word "Pelican" and the depiction of a pelican are trademarks of Arcadia Publishing Company Inc. and are registered in the U.S. Patent and Trademark Office.

Library of Congress Cataloging-in-Publication Data

Ray, T. J., author.
  Side by side : moonshine and murder in Mississippi / by T.J. Ray.
    pages cm
  Includes bibliographical references and index.
  ISBN 978-1-4556-2183-5 (pbk. : alk. paper) — ISBN 978-1-4556-2184-2 (e-book) 1. Mathis, Will, -1902. 2. Murder—Mississippi—Oxford—Case studies. 3. Oxford (Miss.)—History—20th century. I. Title.
  HV6534.O94R39 2016
  364.152'3092276283--dc23
                           2015030524

Printed in the United States of America

Published by Pelican Publishing
New Orleans, LA
www.pelicanpub.com

To Mary Jo Ray, the love of my life

And Cain talked with Abel his brother: and it came to pass, when they were in the field, that Cain rose up against Abel his brother, and slew him.

—Genesis 4:8

Contents

Preface		9
Cast of Characters		11
Chronology		15
Chapter One	The Violent Stage	21
Chapter Two	The Owens Cadre	27
Chapter Three	Blacks, Whites, Ropes	39
Chapter Four	The Moonshine Glow	47
Chapter Five	Life's Contradictions	57
Chapter Six	Pistol Claim Dispute	75
Chapter Seven	Posse Search	89
Chapter Eight	Mathis Eludes the Lawmen	99
Chapter Nine	An Arrest and Its Uproar	113
Chapter Ten	The Judge Faces the Accused	131
Chapter Eleven	The Damning Testimony	147
Chapter Twelve	Whit Owens Faces the Court	165
Chapter Thirteen	Preparing for Hangings	175
Chapter Fourteen	Owens and a New Venue	191
Chapter Fifteen	Father-in-Law Urges Suicide	215
Chapter Sixteen	Side by Side	221
Chapter Seventeen	Justice for White Owens	241
Bibliography		253
Index		254

Preface

Is it pleasant to introduce a story by confessing a myriad of omissions in it? Such is the dilemma facing me at the moment. Let me explain.

Many years ago a very sweet old lady let me read a manuscript someone had sent her. Its author was Marvel Ramey Sisk, its title was Crime Drama in Oxford, Mississippi, and it was dated 1972. The tragedy it depicted in fantastic detail locked my attention and prompted me to look for more about the events of those days in 1901-1902.

Twenty years later someone provided another view of what happened in a document titled A Dastardly Deed, which was "Researched and compiled by: Amil Mask, September, 1995." Not only did Mr. Mask add photos of the time, but he also presented wonderful information about all the trials that resulted from that dastardly deed.

Interest in such a sensational event in a small town doesn't fade away. In 2006, D. H. McElreath, C. L. Quarles, and John Ramey, all local residents, produced "The Last Public Hanging in Oxford," a seventeen-page history.

For nearly three decades my curiosity about that awful day in Oxford and its aftermath kept my attention. I tried to imagine the uproar that the double murders of two federal marshals would cause in the little town—followed by the simultaneous hanging of the two culprits after half a dozen trials. My search resulted in a monstrous pile of scans and photocopies of documents. Finding the court transcripts was a dusty business. Waiting for answers to letters to the Justice Department and the Marshal Service was tedious.

Reviewing reel and after reel of microfilm of old newspapers was fascinating.

In the end, much of what I put on paper had to be scrapped, at the suggestion of an excellent editor. The subsequent happenings in the lives of some main characters would certainly provide another volume.

Through all of the research and rooting around courtroom vaults for transcripts, my sweet wife, Mary Jo, supported me. And she deserves the credit for this book, putting up with my trips to courthouses and all. Sadly, she will not get to hold the book as she passed away in June 2015.

Cast of Characters

Alternate spellings of the names of several individuals appearing in this narrative can be found in the historical record. Those spellings have been preserved whenever quoted and are noted in the following profiles.

J. W. T. Falkner — *One of Orlando Lester's appointed attorneys. Grandfather of William Faulkner.*

John Harkins — *Sheriff of Lafayette County.*

Acting Gov. Harrison — *Approved September 24, 1902, as the ultimate date of the Mathis/Lester hangings.*

William "Bill" Jackson — *Brother of George Jackson. Friend of Will Mathis. Convicted in the murders of John A. Montgomery and Hugh Montgomery and sentenced to life in prison. Spent two years in the state penitentiary.*

George Jackson — *Brother of William "Bill" Jackson. Friend of Will Mathis. Convicted in the murders of John A. Montgomery and Hugh Montgomery. Sentenced to two years in the state penitentiary.*

Walter Jones — *Potential witness against Will Mathis. Involved in Lester's arrest for moonshining. Survived an attempted assassination in September 1901.*

Orlando Lester — *Employee of Whit Owens. Involved in the* murder of Hamp Williams. Hanged for the murders of John A. Montgomery and Hugh Montgomery. Also referred to as Orlanda/Olander/Orlander/Orlandus/Arlandus Luster.

Gov. Andrew Houston Longino — *Governor of Mississippi during most of the trials. Granted Mathis and Lester a respite from the first hanging date to June 1902 and again from that date to September 10, 1902.*

Baxter Cleveland "Clelon" Mathis — *Second son of Will and Cordie Mathis. Named after his uncle, Baxter Clelon Mathis. Also referred to as Clelan.*

Cordelia "Cordie" D. Mathis — *Wife of Will Mathis. Daughter of Whit Owens. Also referred to as Cordia. Last name sometimes spelled "Matthis."*

William Edward "Will" Mathis — *Son of Samuel Mathis of Chickasaw County. Husband of Cordie Mathis. Father of Clelon. Hanged for the murders of John A. Montgomery and Hugh Montgomery. Last name sometimes spelled "Matthis."*

Frank Matthews — *Deputy US marshal.*

P. E. Matthews — *Former sheriff of Lafayette County.*

Dave Montgomery — *Brother of Hugh Montgomery who identified Hugh's watch at the trials.*

Hugh Montgomery — *Deputy US marshal murdered in November 1901. No relation to John A. or M. A. Montgomery.*

John A. Montgomery — *Deputy US marshal murdered in November 1901. No relation to Dave, Hugh, or M. A. Montgomery.*

Cast of Characters

M. A. Montgomery — *US district attorney for Northern District of Mississippi. Referred to as Professor. No relation to Dave, Hugh, or John A. Montgomery.*

Martha "Mat" Owens — *Wife of Whit Owens. Mother of Cordie.*

Whit Owens — *Husband of Martha "Mat" Owens. Father of Cordie Mathis. Father-in-law of Will Mathis. Tried for the murders of Hamp Williams, Hugh Montgomery, and John A. Montgomery. Served seven and a half years of a life sentence.*

Tom Ragland — *Jailer at Lafayette County Jail.*

J. O. "Pete" Ramey — *Deputy sheriff. Father of Marvel Ramey Sisk. Brother-in-law of Sheriff John Harkins.*

W. A. Roane — *District attorney for Lafayette County.*

Dave Rogers — *Deputy US marshal, whom Mathis attempted to murder.*

Hubert D. Stephens — *Son of Z. M. Stephens, whom he assisted in defending Whit Owens.*

Judge Zacariah Marion Stephens — *Hired by Whit Owens to defend him.*

Dan Welch — *Neighbor of Will Mathis, who with his wife, Ellen, and their neighbors, Lonnie Roebuck (sometimes spelled "Robuck") and his wife, discovered the bodies of the Montgomerys.*

Hampton "Hamp" Williams — *Negro accidentally killed in the attempted assassination of Walter Jones.*

Chronology

November 5, 1901 — Hamp Williams is fatally shot. Walter Jones, the intended victim, is wounded.

November 16, 1901 — John A. and Hugh Montgomery are killed.

December 31, 1901 — Special session of circuit court begins for the Montgomery murders. Mathis and Lester are tried and sentenced to hang. William Jackson is sentenced to life in prison. George Jackson is sentenced to two years in prison.

January 9, 1902 — Owens' first trial: Owens is tried for the murder of John A. Montgomery. He is found guilty and sentenced to life in prison. (Appealed.)

January 11, 1902 — Owens' second trial: Owens is tried for the murder of Hugh Montgomery. He is found guilty and sentenced to hang. (Appealed.)

May 1902 — The Mississippi Supreme Court affirmed the Mathis and Lester hangings, set for June 24.

June 9, 1902 — Mississippi State Supreme Court reversed and remanded the verdict against Owens in the John A. Montgomery case of January 9 to a lower court for retrial. The Mathis/Lester executions are stayed to get testimony.

August 18, 1902 — In a special term of circuit court in Holly Springs, Owens is tried for Hugh Montgomery's murder. Gov. Andrew Houston Longino stays the Mathis/Lester executions until September 10. Owens' trial for the murder of Hamp Williams is scheduled for September 11, so a further delay of the Mathis/Lester executions is set until September 24.

September 1–4, 1902 — Owens' third trial: In Holly Springs, Owens is retried for John A. Montgomery's murder. The jury finds Owens guilty and recommends prison time. Not in accord with instructions, they are sent back to reconsider. This time they recommend "him to the mercy of the court," another illegal verdict. Owens is sentenced to life in prison. (Appealed.)

September 11, 1902 — Owens' fourth trial: In a regular term of circuit court, Owens is tried for the murder of Hamp Williams. He is found guilty and sentenced to hang. (Appealed.)

September 24, 1902 — Mathis and Lester are hanged.

March 2, 1903 — Owens' fifth trial: In the Mississippi State Supreme Court retrial for Hamp Williams' murder, Owens' hanging sentence is reversed and remanded. The case against Owens in the Williams murder is sent back to Holly Springs.

September 1903 — In Holly Springs, Owens is retried for the Montgomery murders as ordered by the Mississippi State Supreme Court. Owens is found not guilty of John A. Montgomery's murder. He is not tried again for Hugh Montgomery's murder.

October 31, 1903 — Owens' sixth trial: In a retrial of the Hamp Williams case, Owens is found guilty and sentenced to life in prison. (Appealed, but verdict affirmed.)

January 13, 1912 — Owens is released from prison after seven and a half years.

Side By Side

Moonshine and Murder   **in Mississippi**

Chapter One
The Violent Stage

The Paris Exposition and the new century promised a sparkling vista of what was to come. America had begun to recover from the Civil War. Westward expansion to the Pacific had been accomplished. And the new technology of dynamos and generators and available electric power touted at the fair promised an exciting future. As 1900 dawned, the progress of civilization seemed boundless.

Despite the eyes raised to the horizon, however, changes in the ways of the human heart happen only gradually. For every dress that could be ordered in a Sears, Roebuck catalogue, there was a desperado who thumbed his nose at the feeble grasp of the local sheriff. Side by side with a grand tour of Europe were the gangs of outlaws that populated the Wild West.

In Oxford, Mississippi, those two competing forces would clash after one of the most heinous crimes of that time, or any time, was committed in the nearby countryside. Although race would play a role, the outcome that usually occurred in these cases—a black man lynched by a white mob—was tempered by an odd fact about the main two villains in the case. One was white and one was black. Together they were distilling illegal whiskey and passing off counterfeit money. Each one had been arrested numerous times. After the murders and subsequent harrowing fire took place, one would point the finger at the other and say, "He did it."

Will Mathis and Orlando Lester were half drunk most of the time and free-spirited scofflaws all the time. If they were arrested, they could count on Will's father-in-law,

Whit Owens, to post bail and get them out. Indeed, many of the local residents considered Owens the leader of the moonshining gang. They were a fine pack of scoundrels, doing whatever they pleased and threatening whomever they pleased and devil take the hindmost.

No one could predict, however, that these wild and crazy guys would decide that no one had the right to stop them. When two federal marshals, Hugh and John A. Montgomery, rode out on the afternoon of November 16, 1901, to the house of Will Mathis to arrest him for illegal liquor trafficking, they could have never guessed that they would not see the next dawn. No one, not even Mathis or Lester, had any notion of how their latest clash with the law would turn out.

At this time, Oxford had long been the home of the University of Mississippi, founded in 1848 and commonly known as "Ole Miss." Its long history had begun when the land was originally purchased from the Chickasaw princess Ho-Ka for $800. The town of Oxford was officially chartered on May 11, 1837. In the square at the center of the town, the firm of Gordon and Grayson erected a courthouse to serve as the seat of Lafayette County, turning it over to the county in 1840. During the Civil War, Federal troops under Gen. Ulysses S. Grant passed through on their way south to capture Vicksburg, and in 1864 Gen. Andrew Jackson Smith burned the buildings in the town square, including the county courthouse.

The town slowly rebuilt after the war, and federal judge Robert Andrews Hill arranged funding to erect a new courthouse in 1872. The *Oxford Observer* later described it this way: "The courthouse was magnificent with a majestic cupola and glistening steeple pointing to the clouds; two large porticoes, one north and one south, each supported by four columns and ornamented work. A fence enclosed [an octagonal] yard and ornamental trees."

The city fathers sought to make their town an attractive,

comfortable place in other ways as well. In a history of the county, *The Heritage of Lafayette County, Mississippi*, the Skipwith Historical and Genealogical Society commented on improvements around town: "In 1886, an order was issued that elm shade trees be set out in front of all businesses on the square and down the side streets. . . . [I]n 1889, the Board ordered all merchants and shop keepers to sweep their trash to the rear of the building and deposit it in a barrel which the Marshall would arrange to haul away periodically." In a move to prevent fires from spreading, in April 1890 the Board "recognized the need for an organization to protect the town from fire by passing this resolution, 'on the proper organization of a hook and ladder company by the citizens of this town, the board will equip same.' It was also resolved that 'after this date no one shall be allowed to build a frame building of any kind or put up a wooden roof on any building now standing within 300 feet of the public square of this town.'"

By 1900, Oxford had grown to a small town of 1,825. In the main square, the smaller federal building faced the courthouse from the east, and various hotels and eating places ran around the perimeter. The town's description is furthered in Joseph Blotner's biography of William Faulkner, describing what it looked like in November 1901:

> Facing the Courthouse were the rebuilt stores with balconied second-floor offices that still bore an occasional token of A. J. Smith's visit in 1864. Interspersed among them were the new buildings, such as the one which housed their grandfather's law offices at the northeast corner of the Square. The Bank of Oxford stood at the north end of the Square, the red brick post office to the east, flanked by one-story, iron-awninged Neilson's department store. Among the other business establishments there were drugstores on the south side and a hardware store to the west. There were other stores on North Street and South Street, and above them all soared the almost-new water tank. Bulbous and shining, it stood on thin guy-wired girders, capable of holding 60,000 gallons

of water 140 feet in the air. Here and there oaks and elms shaded the loungers who talked or played checkers outside the Courthouse. The board walk made it possible for shoppers to complete their rounds in unmuddied shoes when it rained. In some of the occasional summer dry spells the trim buggies and slow, loaded wagons would raise clouds of dust as they circled through the unpaved Square.

Blacksmith shops and wagon and carriage shops were ranged down South Street. All types of wagons, buggies, and horses parked on the streets spoked out from the Square or were tied to the hitching rails around the courthouse. In the backs of some wagons were homemade or homegrown goods brought to be sold. Whole families decamped from their creaking vehicles, happy to stretch after many miles on the rutted, sometimes washed-out roads that crisscrossed the county.

It was out in the countryside that Will Mathis plied his criminal trades. He lived in an area south of Oxford known as Delay. Among several suggestions as to why the community was given this name, one holds that a Frenchman named Delay had been a squatter, living with the local Indians before the area became part of Lafayette County in 1840. By the turn of the century, as Joseph Blotner described it, "mostly the houses were scattered, some lining the gravel or clay roads, others back beyond the pastures and cotton fields, still others in the hills where only a pale plume of smoke above the pines would give evidence of life."

The respectable portion of the rural community was terrorized by gangs who banded together in crime, wreaking vengeance on those who provoked their ill will. Clustered within a radius of five miles were a number of tough characters who distilled wildcat whiskey, manufactured counterfeit money, and committed various depredations on the property of their neighbors.

In this lawless area, the officer who ventured into the

neighborhood in search of a felon always took his life in his own hands. Revenue officers discovered that respectable people refused to give them information, and they were more than once told that antagonizing a gang could cost a man his property or his life. This state of affairs had gone on in the Delay neighborhood for a number of years. Upstanding citizens felt this reign of unchecked lawlessness was a reproach to the county, but law officers were powerless to eradicate or even to curb the nefarious activities.

The *Oxford Eagle* commented: "[T]he men who have been operating in that territory did not seem to find in illicit distilling sufficient occupation for their illegal talent, and occasionally resorted to counterfeiting and other crimes to supply the exchequer and the occupation when the proceeds of the still were not deemed sufficiently munificent. As a natural corollary of this sort of business, murder and assassination have flourished as fine arts in the vicinity."

The *Oxford Globe* weighed in as well: "For years, wildcat stills and accompanying evils have existed in LaFayette County and only spasmodic attempts have been made to rid the community of their baleful influence. The effects of this lawlessness is shown in the recent attempt to bring [Will] Mathis to punishment for various crimes. . . . There are more tragedies yet to come, unless heroic efforts are made to clean the county of the lawless element."

"As a natural corollary of this sort of business murder and assassination have flourished as fine arts in the vicinity." Thus wrote a special correspondent to the *Commercial Appeal* in Memphis, Tennessee, in November 1901. The writer had come to Oxford to cover the sensational doings that had stirred the entire region, one not unaccustomed to murders and lynchings but nevertheless shocked by the particularly horrible nature of the crime under investigation.

The reporter went on: "The respectable portion of the community was absolutely terrorized by Mathis, Owens, the Jackson boys and other members of the gang who were banded together in crime, and who knew well how to wreak vengeance on those who were so indiscreet as to provoke their ill will. As a result, the quiescence of the terrorized part of the population combined with the bold and reckless criminality of the moonshining gang to stamp the entire neighborhood with a very lawless character."

Even among his wildcat brethren, Will Mathis had been feared for a long time. He enjoyed a reputation in several nearby counties as a terror in all respects, being absolutely devoid of fear yet crafty and cunning in his criminal deeds, and generally succeeded in effectually covering all his tracks. In order to keep plying his trades freely, he developed a reputation as a brutal character, bullying and threatening his neighbors. People were afraid to feed their stock after dark for fear of being murdered from ambush by this man or his confederates, and "should he be caught they can live in peace. We have heard that several people contemplate leaving that part of the county, as they were in constant dread of something similar to this crime happening to them."

The twin killings of federal marshals would shock the good citizens of Oxford, but what they didn't know was that Will Mathis and his crew had been building toward the desperate crimes for a number of years. As any law enforcement official knows, murderers often start with lesser offenses and, getting away with those, proceed to felonies that are increasingly reckless. The murders of the Montgomerys formed only the capstone of what had been a long and vicious career in crime.

Chapter Two
The Owens Cadre

In 1901, Whit Owens' farm could be found north of the highway that ran west to Oxford and east to Pontotoc. On March 14, 1883, W. B. Roebuck sold 120 acres to Owens' wife, Martha, for $300. This was part of 320 acres of land in a Deed of Trust executed February 17, 1880, by W. B. Roebuck to Wiley Bullard, Martha Owens' father. The 120 acres is the only land Martha or Whit Owens ever owned in the county.

A reporter would describe Owens while he was in jail awaiting one of his many trials: "When the visitor approaches the cell Owens makes a shifty side step like some hunted animal, and it is next to impossible to obtain a square look in his eyes. He is about fifty years of age, has rough brown hair, a small, sandy mustache with a few streaks of gray and dresses in the garb of a rough farmer. He talks with apparent reluctance, and it is difficult to tell whether his reticence is purposeful or due to embarrassment."

An indication of what sort of principles Whit Owens possessed can be seen in the use of his property to gain loans that he never paid back. In 1892, Owens used the land as collateral for a deed of trust executed to William Frasier for a $200 loan from George Morgan. When Owens defaulted on the repayment of the loan, the land was sold to the highest bidder—none other than Whit Owens himself, who bought the land again for $167. He then used the same land as security for the $167 that he had to borrow from the Bank of Oxford.

Later, Owens mortgaged the property twice for a total of $1,000 to hire two of the best lawyers to be found. After that he somehow was able to borrow a second $1,000 on the property. The lawyers were persuasive enough to save him from the gallows that claimed his son-in-law in 1902. No one knows what became of the additional thousand dollars, because it was evidently spent before his trial in Holly Springs. In fact, he had to take an oath of poverty before the court. Unable to repay the note on the farm, he would lose it. The new owner, Arthur Harris, who bought the place from the bank, let Martha and the girls continue to live on it.

Directly next door to the west resided George Mask and his family, and just north of George lived his brother Frank. George had married Whit Owens' eldest of seven daughters, Lorena. The Mask boys' father, John Silas Mask, had fought in the Civil War and then moved to Lafayette County. Both George and Frank and their families would eventually settle in New Mexico.

Will Mathis' wife, Cordie, was the second of Owens' children, born before he acquired the Lafayette County property. A beautiful woman, a number of reporters would comment on her looks. One said, "She is a handsome woman, with skin as soft and white as the skin of a girl," and another commented, "[H]er brown eyes are lustrous and full of expression, her complexion is clear and beautiful, and her even white teeth show clearly behind perfectly formed lips of sensual redness." She and her husband, Will, lived in a house owned by Dan Welch, who also lived nearby. So—almost within shouting distance, certainly within range of the sound of gunfire, and in fairly easy view of one another—were the houses of Will Mathis, Whit Owens, George Mask, and Dan Welch.

A relevant bit of geography helps to fill out the families. West of George Mask lay the Kingdom Cemetery. Over the next three decades, many of the principals in this book would find their final resting place there. Today two rows of notables sleep quietly under the tall pines. In one line are the graves of Baxter Cleveland "Clelon"; the first son of Will and Cordie Mathis; DeWitt C. Weeks and Cordie Mathis,

Whit Owens (7) and family, including Cordie (1) and Martha (8)

Martha Owens and family with George Mask (back left)

Will and Cordie Mathis

sharing a marker; and Will E. Mathis. His grave marker lists his birth as November 22, 1875, and his death as September 24, 1902; his inscription reads "May he rest in Peace." The second row contains the remains of Whit and Martha Owens as well as Marshall, their son. He was born March 8, 1899, and died of whooping cough on February 4, 1901. Next to him was buried Daniel, a baby of Will and Cordie's. He lived only a short time, from February 7 to March 20, 1901. The words at the bottom of his marker read "Our loved one."

Although this neck of the woods would come to inspire terror in their neighbors, the moonshine distillers were not so fearsome in appearance. One reporter who would talk with each of them after their arrests offered this description:

> Picture to yourself the protagonist in this crime: A small man, weighing perhaps 130, with light hair roughened in shocks, a small face, rather weak than otherwise, expressionless grey eyes, which can at times, however, glass in flashes the savage instinct of his ignorant brain, small feet and small hard hands. Formed, one would almost exclaim, to illustrate in the flesh the principle of contrast! When he speaks, it is in a low, gentle tone. When he looks at you his eyes drop as if through diffidence or bashfulness.
>
> His accomplices are of ordinary types and are hardly worth even a passing notice. Whit Owens, his father-in-law, is a man 50 years of age, weighing 155 pounds, is only five feet six inches in height, short, thick neck, blue eyes, brown hair and light moustache.

Unprepossessing as Mathis may have appeared physically, his demeanor and voice belied his wild, explosive, savage nature. To some degree this behavior was driven by his incessant drinking. He had not always been so mean.

When asked to supply some facts about his past life, he related that he was born in Chickasaw County, fifty miles to the southeast, as the son of a farmer. When he was fourteen years of age, he joined the Presbyterian church in

Young Will Mathis

the neighborhood, and for five years he was, according to his statement, a most consistent member. Then he fell in with bad companions and began to make liquor. He bought a fiddle, learned to play it, went to dances, and began to drink a good deal. He moved out of his parents' house at age twenty-one and moved to the Delay neighborhood, wanting to make whiskey there. Soon after his arrival he married the daughter of Whit Owens, who was also engaged in illicit distilling.

"I have been making whiskey for over five years," he said, "and I haven't got as much now as I had when I started. It's all a mistake that there is any money in making whiskey, and I can't understand now why I followed it as long as I did. My wife tried to get me to stop it, and said she would go in the field and plow if I wouldn't have anything more to do with it. You lose about half of the whiskey you make in having to treat all your friends in the country to keep them from giving you away, and what little money you manage to get has to go to the lawyers to get you out of trouble when you are arrested. Then you've got to pay a whole lot of people to keep a lookout for you all the time."

Mathis lived in a section that had long been noted for its lawlessness and mysterious crimes that had demanded attention from both state and federal authorities. Clustered about within a radius of a half dozen miles were a number of hardened characters who distilled wildcat whiskey, manufactured counterfeit money, and committed various depredations on the property of their neighbors in open defiance of the law. Any officer who ventured into the neighborhood in search of a prisoner took his life in his own hands.

While they found no lack of customers for the devil's brew, others were intent on stamping out this commodity, primary among them the Woman's Christian Temperance Union (WCTU). Founded in Ohio and New York in the fall of 1873, this national organization coordinated women who were concerned about the destructive power of alcohol. They met in churches to pray and then called upon their neighbors to desist, on occasion visiting saloons to ask the owners to close up shop. Their activities soon expanded to other areas of moral impropriety. Just before Thanksgiving 1900, the ladies in Oxford launched a crusade against the waxen images used to display the dressmaker's art, because arms and neck were bared. According to the WCTU, "Thrifty husbands should encourage these ladies and insist that these artistic, fascinating—and expensive—creations shall be displayed to the public gaze upon broomsticks."

Except for the dear hearts of the WCTU and their allies,

the people of Lafayette County did imbibe from time to time. And though a bottle of bonded whiskey might cost as little as $2.00, still cheaper booze was to be had, locally made white lightning.

That's what Owens and Mathis produced in great quantities, enough that their illegal activities attracted the attention of the law. In this case, law enforcement was imposed not by the local police but the federal Bureau of Alcohol, Tobacco, Firearms and Explosives. It is the oldest of the tax-collecting agencies in the Department of the Treasury, tracing its roots back to 1789, when Congress imposed a tax on imported spirits to help pay off the debts accumulated during the Revolutionary War. In 1862, Congress created an Office of Internal Revenue, set up to collect taxes on alcohol and tobacco, and the following year Congress authorized enforcement measures to ensure these taxes were collected. More important for Whit Owens and his son-in-law, these officers were also assigned to stop the criminal evasion of taxes.

A measure of how desperate these men were came into full view when two revenue officers went out to arrest Whit Owens. While Will Mathis was in jail later, he dictated his life story to a fellow inmate and gave some of the details of the early run-in with the federal authorities. "In February, 1899, the revenue officers went to Whit Owens' house to capture a still that he and I were running in a large cellar under Owens' smoke house." They rode up to his house one night and called his name. He came to the door in his nightshirt, thinking that someone had come to buy whiskey. Once he found out what they wanted, Genie Anderson, one of the officers, grabbed hold of him.

Saying he wanted to put on some clothes, Owens broke free from Anderson and hurried back toward the front door. The officers told him to halt, but he kept going. They then fired at him, and as he ran inside, his wife slammed the door behind him. Shortly thereafter, he reappeared at a window, a pistol in his hand, and he at once opened fire on the two officers.

At the first shot, Mathis, who lived only four hundred yards away, was alerted by these signs of trouble. According to him, "The officers shot 35 bullet holes through the house while all of his family were inside, his wife and seven children. They kept running around the house screaming all of the time of the shooting, the clothes hanging in the house were shot into holes."

Immediately, Mathis ran toward his father-in-law's house, closely followed by his wife. He had a gun in his hand, and his wife is said to have had a pistol under her apron. They almost ran over the two officers, who shot at Mathis as he broke boldly through the line of fire and gained entry into the house. With these reinforcements, and with every indication of a desperate and perhaps bloody resistance, the officers deemed it best to desist.

"The officers started to leave, and were going through the house. Owens went to a back window and began firing on them again. They fired back but kept going. After they got off Owens told me to help the women to move the still out of the smoke house. He guarded the house, and we moved the still off, and then carried off about 20 gallons of whiskey Owens had in the house. We then poured out the beer in the lot. Owens turned the hogs in to eat up the meal that was in the beer, and root it up in the dirt so it could not be detected. We then hauled off the beer stand and pumped the cellar full of water."

This time they were able to escape prosecution. As Mathis related, "We came to Oxford, made bond but the grand jury failed to find any bill, so we got off of that charge. Ever since then Owens has proved a giant to the revenue officers, and has waylaid the roadside every time he knew them to be in the county."

The first brush with the revenue officers seemed to whet their lawless instincts. The moonshiners resorted more to concealment and subterfuge. They also conceived an implacable hatred of all revenue officers. Owens and Mathis were said to have sworn to make an example of someone, which would deter the officers from coming out there in the future.

That explains the attempt to assassinate Deputy Marshal Dave Rogers that fall. In Mathis' autobiography he told what happened:

> In November, 1899, Owens heard the officers were coming to get a still that we had; he got George Mask (his son-in-law) and I [sic] to go out to the still. When we got there it was dark; we found a hickory stump on fire near the still. Owens saw the sparks flying up; he thought it was the officers striking matches around the still. He and Mask had shot guns, I had a winchester. They shot at the sparks about 6 times, I never shot at all, I was to shoot when the officers fired so I could see the blaze of their guns. But we found out soon there were no officers there to shoot.

The threat of the law had them constantly on edge, as an incident the next year shows. Mathis wrote:

> In the fall of 1900, I went with 4 other men to Whit Owens' to get some whiskey. When we got there we found Owens and the negro each armed with a breech loading shot gun.
> They halted us, said they were looking for the officers that night. We got our whiskey and left as soon as we could. Orlander Lester and Bill Jinins [a brother-in-law of Lester's] were the negroes that were with Owens.
> After the boys and I got back to my house we decided to sit up awhile and see if we could hear any shooting down at Owens', so we killed a chicken, cooked and eat [sic] it.
> It was about 12 o'clock when we heard four big guns fire in the direction of Owens'. We were certain the officers had come and they had gotten into a fight. One of the boys and I mounted our horses and rode down there to see if any one [sic] had gotten hurt, but found the crowd was breaking up, and had only fired their guns for sport.

They continued their operations and were subjected to occasional visits from the deputy marshals, but the officers found it impossible to secure the necessary evidence to catch them at their lawless occupation.

During one of these visits a new member joined their organization, one who would prove to play a crucial role in the 1902 murders. The inclusion of Orlando Lester in the gang showed that the love of money cares not about the color of the skin. Although Mathis might refer to him as "the darky," he and Whit Owens came to count on the African American as a fellow conspirator.

The same reporter who described Mathis and Owens had this to say: "The negro, Orlandus Lester, is about 21 years old, tall and heavily built, with a black, unintelligent face." As ensuing trials proceeded, however, it would emerge that Lester was quite intelligent, probably more than Will Mathis. He would in time write a lengthy document about his own life and times, a document that unfortunately has not survived.

Lester first became involved with Whit Owens when he helped defend the Owens family during a raid by federal revenue agents. In 1898, he grabbed a white girl, and after his victim identified him, officers arrested him and put him in jail, where he stayed for eight months. Finally, Owens paid the bail bond for him, employed a lawyer, and got him out of his trouble. Shortly after that, Lester was arrested for distilling, and again Owens came to his rescue. Early in March 1900, the docket of the upcoming circuit court appeared in the papers, and one item listed for the spring term of court was Case #2777, *State v. Orlando Lester*, for assault and battery. Although the outcome of this case is not known, presumably his good angel came to his rescue yet again. Since that time Lester had become a loyal follower, almost a servant to Owens.

This merger between the races threatened to add a special edge to the revenue officers' efforts to stop the moonshining activities of Whit Owens and Will Mathis. The turn of the last century was the heart of the Jim Crow era, where African Americans in the South suffered more than the indignities of separate schools, separate restaurants, and separate facilities. They were also actively persecuted by whites still furious that their former slaves had been freed by Northerners determined to make the South pay for the War Between the States. That resentment tainted every aspect of life, from general social disapproval all the way to its most abhorrent expression: spontaneous lynchings.

Chapter Three
Blacks, Whites, Ropes

The fear of lynching would play a large role in the Will Mathis saga, and he became afraid for a very good reason. When others in his gang were arrested, his wife, Cordie, was swept up in the law enforcement net. That meant she was taken to the same jail as Orlando Lester. So when Mathis heard rumors that the townspeople were fired up enough to lynch, he had good reason for wanting to prevent such lynchings from happening at all costs. Orlando Lester and anyone with him would be only the latest victims of the vigilante killings that were raging through the former Confederacy.

The feelings that whites held toward slaves had not changed much during the generation that had passed since the Civil War. The most famous example in 1900 occurred in the city of Atlanta. Controversy erupted when members of the Grand Army of the Republic protested the use of school books that pictured the federal government in a bad light and included a history of the Civil War sympathetic to the Confederacy. In the South, sympathy for the cause still held sway. The former rebels had been dismissed from a failed army, but they came home to open arms.

A review of scattered local news reports shows many of these common attitudes. In February 1900, the *Oxford Globe* expressed alarm at the number of Negroes allowed to "walk the public streets with a case of smallpox. Yesterday morning a negro stepped into Dr. Isom's office, with a bad case of the disease, and wanted to know what was the matter with him." Such effrontery offended the paper's editor, who observed, "Now this won't do. Whoever's duty it is to attend to such should have these negroes isolated, and that quick."

In mid-June, the *Globe* opined: "Negro loafers are getting too cussed numerous. The streets are crowded with them. To tell the truth, the black rascals don't want to work. It is almost impossible to hire one. And then too cooks are getting so they don't want to work. Now they get their living some where [sic] and we don't think it would be a bad idea to rigidly enforce the vagrant law."

The *Globe* often cited the problem of finding good help and, in the process, reducing the number of loafers around the town. "You may look around here all day for a negro laborer and never find one, yet the town is chuck full of loafers of this color. Can't there be some city legislation enacted to get in behind the vagrants? The farmers need laborers, the town needs laborers, and there is always an opening for laborers, and the vagrants should be made to go to work, both white and black, or leave the burg. There is nothing that gives a bigger black eye to a thriving city than a pack of idlers."

In December, the *Oxford Eagle* weighed in on the same topic:

> Nature is a model of economy of forces, and has made no provision for an idler's existence, except when aided and abetted by the genus homo. As individuals and as communities, we might profit by the lessons daily taught us in the great free school of life.
>
> Almost every day may be seen standing upon our corners, and loafing around the public square, dozens of able bodied men and boys, who apparently have no object in life except to kill time. Some of these idlers are useless, lazy negroes, who tramp the streets by day to select what they may steal at night. The only difference is, the white men and boys live by somebody else's labor and the negroes exist by crap-shooting or theft. Why not, we would like to ask, practice social and political economy, by putting these idlers to work, and at the same time stop the petty larcenies, so annoying to our hard-working, honest citizens?

From the widespread discrimination rose two camps that espoused different responses. One former Virginia slave, Booker Taliaferro Washington, counseled his fellow blacks that they were better off working with the system they faced. In 1895 he said, "The wisest among my race understand that the agitation of questions of social equality is the extremest folly."

Other African Americans thought that Washington's position had given license to continued patterns of racial segregation and discrimination. One of those voices was that of W. E. B. Du Bois, who had been educated at Harvard and become a professor of economics, history, and sociology. Du Bois opposed Washington's gradualism, maintaining that such accommodation would lead to further "humiliation and inferiority for blacks." At one time he witnessed the brutal burning of a black, whose knuckles were later displayed in a local drugstore. Du Bois saw that radical means were necessary to gain equality for his people. His efforts led to the formation of the National Association for the Advancement of Colored People.

Shortly after the Civil War, the Radical Republicans had installed a large number of former slaves in positions of political power. The hatred that this aroused among whites guaranteed a swift reversal once the last federal troops were withdrawn from the South in 1877. By March 1901, the *Omaha World-Herald* observed, "There is but one negro in congress now, a negro named White, who was elected from North Carolina. It is safe to say that he will be the last negro congressman for some time to come. His time expires next month. It is interesting to recall that the only negroes elected to either House or Senate have come from Southern States. It is of further interest to note that the Republican party, which loves the negro so dearly about election time, never elected a negro senator from a Northern State." The *Oxford Globe* felt this observation was worth repeating.

Indeed, the simmering distrust between the races sometimes exploded in mass hostility. In New Orleans, race riots in July 1900 caused the destruction of many black schools and homes. August brought more racial turmoil. In New York City, the death of a policeman following a scuffle with an African American set off racial violence. The *New York Times* reported, "Every trolley car passing up or down Eighth Avenue was stopped and every negro on board was dragged out and beaten."

In the poisonous atmosphere that permeated every community, a recurrent theme was calling on the police to restrain the former slaves. In December 1900, the *Oxford Globe* offered this opinion: "The latest dash of the trifling negroes is to steal the horses of different families out at night and take in the country picnics. In the last week there has [sic] been more than two dozen horses stolen out and used for this purpose. Someone should catch the black rascals and take a club and whale the face off of them. The black devils are getting too gay here lately anyway."

To a certain degree, African Americans of the time did break the law. While they walked the streets as citizens, they occupied the very bottom of the social and economic ladders. A wage of two cents an hour that set off a massive strike in Puerto Rico was more than many blacks were making. And even when they earned some money, it was often spent in company stores, a recycling of wealth that left the land owners in almost the same position that slave holders had occupied during the antebellum period.

Those who, like Orlando Lester, saw no other recourse would resort to crime. In mid-December, Mr. Tom Denton, while returning home on horseback one Friday night, was held up by three Negroes three miles west of Oxford. They demanded his money and in the scuffle used a knife on him, slicing into his overcoat. Denton was not to be cowed so easily. He also raked out his blade and succeeded in cutting one and bluffing the others. The Negroes ran, with "no clew" on Denton's part as to who they were. The news article supposed they believed Denton had sold his cotton and held him up for his money.

The next month the *Eagle* reported the following confrontation:

> As Mr. A. M. Winter was driving to Oxford in a buggy Saturday morning in company with a young lady, three miles west of town he was accosted by two negroes, Will and Noah Sanders, who drew a pistol and threatened to shoot Mr. Winter. Without noticing their insulting language and threats, Mr. Winter whipped up his horse and escaped without injury.
>
> He reported the assault to the town officials who promptly proceeded to the home of the negroes and arrested them. They were given a preliminary trial before Justice T. L. Harris Saturday afternoon and bound over to appear before his Honor next Saturday.

These arrests were none too gentle, depending on who made them. In September, the *Eagle* reported the following theft: "W. D. Moore and Robert Ivy, a negro, of the Splinter neighborhood, were arrested Saturday night by Messrs. J. M. Tatum, J. B. Roach and a posse of citizens and placed in jail Sunday morning for having a mule, known to have been stolen from parties in Grenada county in their possession. Moore was released from jail on Monday morning upon giving a bond of $500 for his appearance before Squire T. L. Harris this morning. The negro was painfully, but not dangerously wounded."

Yet loafing and stealing were only petty crimes. When crimes of a more serious nature occurred, many communities did not wait for the police to catch the culprits. Instead, the townsfolk would appoint themselves judge, jury, and executioner. During this era, Mississippi would lead the nation in the number of lynchings that occurred within its boundaries.

In November 1900, for example, the *Commercial Appeal* in Memphis, Tennessee, carried a story about an incident in Gulfport, Mississippi, that was one more in a sad continuum of brutal justice:

> Negro Burned at the Stake
> Almost Murdered and Criminally Assaulted White Woman.
> Swift and Awful Penalty
> Posse Soon Overhauled the Fugitive, Whose Identification Was Followed by Confession—Conviction and Sentence by Informal Court.

Just over a month later the swift hand of vigilante justice would strike again. Newspapers headlined terrible deeds. The first one given was run by the *Globe*:

> Wholesale Lynching.
> Lawrence County, Mississippi, the Scene of the Hangings.
> Story of the Identification of the Negro Murderer and the Pleas in His Behalf. The Husband Father of the Victims Lifts His Voice Against Summary Punishment.
> Wesson, Dec. 9.—One of the most atrocious and inhuman murders ever heard of was committed last night in the edge of Simpson county, some twenty miles from here.
> Brown Smith, a farmer, left his family at his home in the country to go to town for shopping purposes, thinking of no possible danger to them. This morning when he returned he found his wife and five children weltering in their blood, and apparently all dead.
> One of the little girls, supposed this morning to have been dead, has revived enough to tell what she knew of the occurrence. She said she knows the man who committed the deed; that it was a negro, and described him.
> It is greatly feared that a wholesale lynching may take place in that neighborhood, as the county is excited to the highest pitch.
>
> Wholesale Lynching.
> Wesson, Miss., Dec. 11.—A gentleman named McBride, who

left the scene of the murder of the Smith family, twenty miles east of here, at 2 o'clock this afternoon, has just reached here. Mr. McBridge says a mob of 1,000 men has formed, and that a wholesale lynching is taking place in that neighborhood.

Lynching at Lewis.
Brookhaven, Miss. Dec. 11. . . . After capturing Charley Lewis, the alleged murderer, the mob placed him alongside several other negroes and asked the little girl, who escaped the murderer, to pick out the one who killed her mother. She at once pointed to Lewis. This strong evidence to the mob made it difficult for Sheriff Gassell, of Monticello, to induce the people to turn Lewis over to him for safekeeping. He assured them he would have the negro at Bankston Ferry yesterday morning at 10 o'clock for trial.

As promised, he arrived there on time with Lewis, and another mob of two hundred men, armed with shotguns and Winchesters, met him on the opposite bank of the river.

Speeches were made by cool-headed men, among them being Hon. A. F. Weathersby, senator from Lawrence county, and Rev. Drummons, a Methodist preacher, who pleaded eloquently for the negro's life.

An Unexpected Plea.
Brown Smith, the man whose family was murdered, and who should, of course, have felt the most aggrieved, got upon the water-shelf of the little store gallery and pleaded with the crowd to be patient and not to rush hastily into a thing they might regret. He said that while he did not doubt his child's word, yet she was so young there was a possibility that she might have been mistaken. He said there was something there (pointing to his left breast) which did not exactly satisfy him about the matter.

. . . After parleying for some time the mob, under the leadership of a few determined men, made a rush for the negro and succeeded in getting him from the deputies after a hard struggle. They put a plow line around the negro's neck and ran up the hill with him. He was put on a big black horse and driven under a tree. After the halter was fastened to a limb the horse was driven from under him. His feet touched the ground, but he was strangling, and Mr. Arrington, one of the lawyers, and another man, cut him down. He would not speak. The crowd allowed him to be revived and then hung him in earnest. His body was left hanging by the roadside. Lewis denied his guilt to the last.

The crimes committed by Will Mathis and his gang took place during these days of the terrifying, self-appointed *posse comitatus*. Lynchings and burnings were becoming so commonplace that Congress and various state legislatures were beginning to talk of laws that would lead to the prosecution of those who took the law into their own hands. As wild as the moonshiners were, they had seriously raised the stakes of a deadly game when they brought Orlando Lester within their midst. As events would develop, Mathis would try to use Lester in the familiar role of scapegoat. Yet Lester himself was not shy about making his own claims. In the end, the outcome would be a plague on both their races.

Chapter Four
The Moonshine Glow

With Orlando Lester on board, the Mathis moonshine gang entered a new, more reckless phase. Not content with producing only liquor, Will Mathis tried his hand at counterfeiting. When anyone dared protest, the gang went after the potential witnesses. Not surprisingly, they were attracting more and more pressure from the authorities. Yet despite the fact that they kept being arrested, they managed to stay out of jail because of their intimidation practices. Their very success with this tactic would lead them to a dangerous conclusion: that officers of the law could be treated like ordinary citizens.

They had a good run for a couple of years. Like other moonshiners, a major reason that they could succeed despite the number of charges leveled against them was a lack of witnesses at their trials. This held true even for preliminary grand jury proceedings. At the end of March 1900, a report of the grand jury was sent to the Hon. Z. M. Stephens, judge of the Third Judicial District, Oxford, Mississippi. It read, in part:

> The whiskey sellers of the county in the main are fine judges of human nature and sell whiskey only to men who will swear falsely when they come before the Grand Jury. We are perfectly satisfied that the only way to break up the blind tigers of the county is for the good men who oppose the unlawful sale of liquors to make affidavit before the Justices of the Peace and search for and seize liquors kept for sale and find out who are in possession of U. S. internal revenue license. The amount of perjury in the county is absolutely appalling.
> It is humiliating to have to make this but we feel constrained to tell your honor of these unpleasant truths. The Grand Jury

has been diligent and earnest but our labors have almost been vain.

Intimidating possible witnesses in turn led to further arrests. On August 8, 1900, around nine o'clock at night, Dave Rogers, who lived six miles from Oxford on the Delay road, was in bed playing with his baby when someone fired a shot from a .44 rifle through the window at him. The bullet fortunately missed its victim and lodged in the mattress. The sheriff was at once notified, and Deputy Pete Ramey left immediately for the scene.

A week later, Will Mathis and neighbor John Welch were arrested and charged with the shooting. The evidence against them was only circumstantial, but they were ordered to appear at a preliminary trial the following week.

By September the circuit court docket included the trial of Will Mathis, who had paid bail after his hearing, for shooting with intent to kill one Dave Rogers. The nine witnesses against him included Rogers himself and none other than John Welch, who apparently turned state's witness. Yet at the end of the session the court respectfully referred the case to the next grand jury, as "we failed to get all the witnesses." This would not be the end of the matter. When the case came before a new grand jury, however, the witnesses against Mathis had been reduced to merely John and Edgar Welch, and no bill of indictment was handed up to the court.

The efforts of the revenue officers continued. In December, the law succeeded in running down one of the "blind tigers." United States Marshals Butler, Montgomery, and Rogers went out the first Saturday twelve miles south of town and captured a still of about sixty gallons' capacity. None of the operators were caught.

Will Mathis' activities accelerated the following summer. Hot weather created thirst, and as always, the moonshiners were accommodating enough to serve their fellow citizens' need. Their stills were among many in the quiet, wooded glens in the county that crackled and gurgled with the sound of oak chips burning under pots filled with corn mash, making its way through a set of coils to emerge as white lightning.

In late July, on a stifling hot Saturday night, the folks enjoying themselves at Springdale Church in the southeastern section of the county were entertained by Will Mathis. Hiram Pilcher, unfortunately, was on the receiving end of an assault that included brandishing a pistol at him in a "rude and angry manner not in necessary self defense."

The grand jury in the case heard testimony by Pilcher and a handful of other people in attendance, and it quickly returned an indictment against Mathis, who at that time was at large. The same jury also indicted Mathis on a charge of disturbing the peace during the same event "by loud talking and cursing near the church and exhibiting a pistol." In further business, the grand jury indicted Mathis for carrying a concealed weapon at the homes of John Welch and J. E. Franklin near the church.

Mathis was hardly daunted by the triple charges. Instead, always strapped for cash, he would try to create some that was not government-sanctioned. A recurring problem in many parts of the country during this era was counterfeiting. The poor quality of legal tender was not hard to duplicate, and many cheats found ways to pass off bogus money, both coin and paper, on unsuspecting gullible souls.

Mathis himself told the story as part of his life's history that was sold later by the *Oxford Eagle*: "In the Summer of 1901 Will Stripling got me to come to Oxford and get mettle to make counterfeit money. He said we would make it on halves. I got enough to make $60.00 or $80.00, I got about 40 dollars. After thinking over it I got afraid to use it, I showed it to a friend one day, he said if I was afraid to pass it, if I would let him have it he would pass it." Will proceeded to hand over several dollars of the illegal tender. Although he warned his friend to be careful about passing it, the other desperado said that he did not care. He didn't mind fleeing the state if necessary.

Will continued with the story: "I was with him one day and he got up a game of cards, the one he was playing with wanted to play across, Pruett asked me to be his partner in the game, I told him I would play with him but would not take any part in the betting, he said all right he would do all the betting, he passed the counterfeit money on the boys he was playing with, they found it out and began telling it that Pruett and I passed a lot of bad money on them, it made me mad, I got on my horse and went to see the boys, and gave one of them a thrashing, should have given the other one the same, but he got away. They made out papers against me for passing bad money on them. They also got papers against Pruett, he swore he borrowed five dollars from me, spent it and gave the remainder back to me.

"I was bound over in court until the grand jury found a bill against me. The grand jury found one against Pruett also."

When the authorities were informed that Mathis had found a new outlet for his talents in counterfeiting, the proper steps were taken for his detention. They soon secured samples of the lead dollars that he was distributing around with a liberal hand in the rural district. Finally Mathis was arrested.

As it turned out, he had company for the trip to Oxford. At the same time, the officers arrested Orlando Lester for making whiskey. Another black man named Walter Jones had notified them about Lester's illegal activities and had him arrested. In fact, the twin arrests were more related than the officers thought. Many months later, Walter Jones would state that he had let it be known that he had some of the counterfeit money that Mathis made in his possession. That led to a warning that he might be shot if he testified—a warning the gang would act upon shortly.

Hugh Montgomery was one of the officers for the

counterfeiting arrest. Mathis claims that while he was in custody, he was mistreated by Montgomery. The officer also took away his pistol and refused to return it when Mathis was released. To his general hatred of revenue officers was added a motive of personal revenge for a fancied injury. In time he would comment, "If Hugh Montgomery had treated me right when he arrested me on that counterfeiting charge several months ago, he would be alive today."

On August 12, 1901, Will Mathis was tried before US Commissioner R. S. Adams for making and passing counterfeit dollars and quarters, and for intimidating witnesses. When the grand jury met, they found five different people on which Pruett had passed counterfeit money. So that amounted to five charges—more than enough to send him to prison. The felons were placed under a bail bond of $2,000 each until they could appear at the next term of the federal court.

In the meantime, the revenuers scored another victory. On the 20th, they finally put one of Will Mathis' moonshine plants out of commission. US Marshals Montgomery and Rogers journeyed out in the backwoods and captured a large still. It was located only two hundred yards from the house where Will Mathis lived. Even though he was in jail, the still was said to be his. "It never rains but what it pours," one newspaper editor observed. This would make "eight charges they will have against him."

The felons were not to be stopped, however. In what was becoming a familiar pattern, Whit Owens raised the money for the bail of both his son-in-law and Lester, and the two were released until their court appearances. Their release would prove to be a fatal mistake, because a few weeks later a potential witness against them would be shot. An unlucky bystander would be killed.

In mid-September, a stir went through the community. Here is how one paper reported the event: "At a colored festival near LaFayette Springs, Tuesday night, Hamp Williams was killed and Walter Jones badly wounded. All the participants in the riot were negroes." Yet no other paper made no mention of the shooting—because the stir was minor. No one was arrested and no trial resulted from the murder.

At the coroner's inquest the next day, five buckshot were noted to be in Williams' body: one in the hip, one in the side, one in the right arm, and two in the shoulder blade near the center of his back. The question for the authorities was: Who fired the shotgun? Although witnesses at the scene felt that the shooter was Orlando Lester, why he did it has caused confusion in the record.

The person behind the conspiracy to murder is not entirely clear. According to one version, shortly after they returned home, Mathis and Lester began to scheme to remove the evidence against them. Walter Jones had worked a while for Will Mathis, making sorghum molasses and gathering corn, after he had appeared before the federal grand jury. He was also the main witness in the counterfeiting case. For this reason the two men agreed to kill him.

Lester, who appears to have been a pliant instrument of murder in the hands of Mathis, readily accepted the commission and picked his time for the murder. On the night of the Negro festival, Lester waited in ambush outside the church where the party was going on. Around eight o'clock, Jones, George Dennis, and George Woods stepped outside to answer a call of nature. Before going back inside, they stopped by some bushes while Dennis searched around for a bottle he had stashed there. As Dennis bent down to look for the bottle, Lester fired a charge of buckshot at Jones, almost cutting off his arm and seriously wounding him. Yet part of the charge missed Jones and instead killed an innocent man, Hamp Williams, who was walking in the shadows and was invisible from the position in which the assassin stood.

Will Mathis would declare in his autobiography, however, that he had no connection with the killing. Here is how he recounted the particulars of the murder: "The second Tuesday night in September the negroes had a church festival. Owens stopped work that evening, gave Lester a lot of buck shot, sent him to George Mask for his gun. Owens told him to go through the woods and get to the church about dark, hide himself in a good place so he could shoot and kill a negro named Walter Jones, who had Lester arrested, and billed for making whiskey." Note that in this version, Mathis connected Jones with Lester for his moonshining activities rather than stating any connection to the counterfeiting case.

Mathis went on: "Lester did as Owens told him, when Walter Jones came to the church and walked out to one side to take a drink of wine, he was in a few feet of Lester, he fired at him, Jones turned around as he fired, most of the load hit Hamp Williams, a negro, and killed him dead, 4 shot hit Jones in the shoulder. They had a coroner's inquest over the body of Hamp Williams; the negroes swore there was not a white man on the grounds, that a negro did the shooting, also said they saw the bulk of him and it looked about the size of Lester, and they believed it was him but could not be sure of it."

Using Lester as the instrument of revenge in this case made good sense, since a white person at an all-black gathering would have been noticed by anyone there. Then Mathis claimed he was the one who suffered because of an alleged connection to Jones:

"On the 16th of November U.S. District Attorney Montgomery made out papers against me for selling whisky, he came to arrest me and take me to Oxford and get out papers against me for killing Hamp Williams and shooting Walter Jones, something that I did not have anything to do with at all."

This version Mathis would stick with throughout the court trials that would shortly follow. He claimed the idea was his father-in-law's, not his. "The next day I heard it and went to the church where the dead negro was and saw him. I went down to Whit Owens' the next day and he and Lester told me that Lester did it, and if anybody said anything to me about it for me to tell them that Lester was in the bed sick that night; that Mr. Owens told me that Lester had a chill about 2:00 o'clock and had to stop work, and Mr. Owens went down to his house that night after supper to see how he was and found him in the bed with a high fever, and I knew that Lester didn't kill the negro."

That version would be corroborated by Orlando Lester. In Whit Owens' second trial for this murder, M. A. Montgomery would recall Lester's testimony from the first trial:

> He said that he got the shells from Whit Owens and started by dark, probably a little after dark, to the [church] under the direction of Mr. Owens to go there before it was entirely dark and secrete himself near the [church], there to kill Walter Jones. He said he went there and located himself some distance from the church and looked and didn't see Walter; saw a number of persons and finally saw Walter come out on the smooth ground next to the church into the edge of the woods; somebody else was with him, and that he thought at the time he got there—no, he didn't know who the other person was, but shot at Walter one shot and went away. He said he went back to Whit Owens and reported what he had done, and was asked by Whit if he had killed the party, he said he didn't know; he took the gun back to George Mask's, and then the next morning he heard of the killing of Hamp Williams. He also said there that there was an arrangement made, by which Whit Owens and Mathis would say that in case he was charged with it, that he was at home sick; sick in bed that night.

The killing created considerable excitement, but there were enough extenuating circumstances to convince many people that Mathis was implicated in the killing—to remove a witness against him. The county officers went out and investigated, however, but did not secure enough physical or eyewitness evidence to make any arrests. They simply did not have the minimum required to connect either Mathis or Lester with the crime.

This successful crime still further confirmed Mathis and his accomplice of their own invincibility and astuteness. This arrogance prepared the way for their last crime together—when this illusion would be decisively banished.

At the same time, though, Will Mathis had to be plenty nervous in the aftermath of the murder investigation. When United States Deputy Marshals Hugh and John A. Montgomery came out a week later to arrest him on another moonshining charge, Mathis knew that he was under suspicion of murder. He believed that the arrest for the whiskey violation was merely a blind for their real purpose: to nail the murder on him while they had him in their custody.

Mathis was so apprehensive of being arrested on this latter charge that he went to Walter Jones and by intimidation extorted from him a written statement that he did not believe that Mathis had been in any way connected with the murder of Hamp Williams and the attempted assassination of himself.

The wild spree of the Mathis gang was reaching its violent conclusion. All of their previous crimes were leading up to what happened to the Montgomerys on November 16. Will Mathis' hatred for the officers with whom he had had brushes on more than one occasion; the malice personally felt for Deputy Hugh Montgomery; the fear of being implicated in felony murder; the confidence engendered by past experience that he could commit almost any crime and dupe the officers involved and bulldoze the neighborhood into silence—all these circumstances worked together to urge him forward to the commission of a terrible crime, which was to prove a fitting finale to his criminal career.

Chapter Five
Life's Contradictions

In the town of Oxford, citizens went about their usual chores on that Saturday, November 16. Unlike the desperadoes out in the countryside, people in town were by now enjoying certain modern amenities. The summer before, the executive board of the University of Mississippi had met to consider bids, plans, and specifications for electric lights, steam heating, etc. They appropriated the sum of $2,200 to cover the project.

The vote was a surprise to even the most ardent supporters of such modernization, as there had been considerable talk in opposition. As one local journalist concluded, "With the lights and sewerage system, Oxford will now take its place where she rightly belongs, in the front ranks of the progressive towns in the State, and we predict that in the near future the people of Oxford will enjoy the luxury of electric cars."

Indeed, the superintendent of the Electric System, W. H. Harvey, took out a notice in the newspapers to all Electric Light consumers: "For 60 days, beginning Sept. 26, we will wire all houses (open work) free and a slight charge for concealing wiring. Wall switches, chandeliers and double circuits will be charged for extra." The new year saw the fulfillment of old dreams. On the last Friday of January, the electric current was turned on, "and our streets were for the first time in the history of the town lighted by electricity."

One other advance in utilities would play a more prominent role in the events that transpired over the course of the next two days. The winter before, W. H. Harvey announced in the paper that he had bought out the Oxford Telephone Exchange and that all additional phones then wanted would be put in by the first of April. He assured the town that service would be greatly improved, and long-distance connections would be made in the near future. One was to reach all the way to Holly Springs—thirty miles to the north.

The phone line fortunately extended south to Delay. That meant a good citizen could call Oxford police on the morning of the 17th to report that a horrific crime had been committed. Law enforcement officers would be promptly dispatched to go capture the killers.

One of them was Pete Ramey, a deputy sheriff who worked for his brother-in-law, Sheriff John Harkins. For that reason his daughter, Marvel Ramey, had personal cause to remember the day. Seventy years later, Marvel wrote of that day that began so peacefully:

> Oxford ladies who braved the Saturday crowds for necessary shopping alighted from their buggies, or "run-abouts", and stepped gingerly across the cindered streets, lifting their long skirts modestly below high-top shoe level. . . . Shoppers who consulted the weekly *Oxford Eagle* for November bargains found that the J. E. Neilson Co., Established 1830, advertised fine Millenery. The Oxford Dry Goods Co. offered Ken's All-Wool Suits and Overcoats that "pulverize all competition" at $10.00 and $12.50; Men's and Ladies' Shoes at $1.50 per pair; and subscriptions to *McCall's Magazine* at fifty cents a year.

In his biography of William Faulkner, Joseph Blotner painted his own picture of what town life on a typical Saturday was like:

> There on the Square the merchants in their stores would wait for the Saturday crowds. Outside, drawn up in a great ring around the Courthouse fence would be wagons from the county, piled high with watermelons, tomatoes, corn, or whatever happened to be in season. After shopping at the dry-goods store a woman might pay a visit to one of the drugstores or confectionaries. Her husband, meanwhile,

might poke around at the hardware store, talk to some of his cronies leaning against the Courthouse, and then idle away more time in conversation while he waited his turn in the crowded barbershop on the northwest corner of the Square. If he wanted a drink, he would need to step into a secluded spot with friends who would provide one. He might even seek out a "blind tiger" where he could get a powerful shot of colorless whiskey made from local corn.

That was precisely the reason a small cadre of men were preparing to serve an all-too-familiar warrant. US Deputy Marshal Frank Matthews was about to send two officers, Hugh and John A. Montgomery, on a mission. They were to ride on horseback twelve miles southeast that afternoon to arrest Will Mathis on a charge of illicit distilling. Hugh Montgomery was a field deputy marshal; John was a special deputy, going along with Hugh as his guard. Marshals had been mistreated in that neighborhood before—as Hugh knew very well, since he had been one of them.

The unpaved road the two officers followed went eventually to Pontotoc, nearly thirty miles to the east, where Hugh Montgomery and his family lived. In an old community not far from the Yocona River bottoms, a number of families (Owens and Mask and McElreath and Hogans and Stripling) dated back to the original white settlement of the area. As they took a narrower road south from this sprinkling of houses, the next community was Delay, and to the east a bit farther lay the Dallas community.

The two Montgomerys left Oxford between two and three o'clock and arrived in the Yocona community around four. When they drew near the assigned neighborhood, their first stop was at the home of Dan Welch. He wasn't at home when they arrived, but his wife, Ellen, was. She was acquainted with John but not with Hugh. At a trial several months later, she would testify that the reason they had come calling was to leave a summons for her husband. John Alex, as Mrs.

John A. Montgomery (far right) with his brothers

Welch referred to him, entered the house to get some water.

At the same time he asked directions and the distance to the Mathis place, which Mrs. Welch said was a quarter mile away. Later, when she was asked on the witness stand if she knew whether the marshals reached their destination, she remembered seeing John A. Montgomery arrive there on his black horse. The houses were so close, she said, that at times they could hear the Mathis baby crying. Later that night, she would report seeing the sky lighted by a burning house. She didn't know then that the house on fire was owned by none other than her husband, Dan.

Exactly what happened after dark on that cold Saturday night will never be known. All of the survivors of the horror told versions that slightly or greatly diverged, each motivated by his self-interest or interest in a loved one. That's not to mention the confusion that often occurs when a witness has to recall events on several different occasions. Reports told one day to one jury might be contradicted in a later testimony. Details given in idle conversation between jail cells or overheard from the street outside the jail created even more alternate accounts. In spite of these contradictions, however, the overall sequence that ended on a gallows many months later can be set forth.

That afternoon, Will Mathis had slaughtered a hog and was cleaning it as it hung from a limb behind the house. The first freeze of the year normally came around Thanksgiving, making that the best time for slaughtering hogs. The creature would be scalded in a boiling tub and then cut into pieces and salted down to cure, with some of it ground for sausage. The fat was used to render lard. Often the women would clean and cook the chitterlings or tripe.

Mathis was in the middle of this day-long affair when Hugh and John Montgomery rode up to the house. Helping Mathis were Bill Jackson, a friend of his, and Orlando Lester. Cordie Mathis saw the officers out front first, and she called out to her husband. Mathis circled the small house to meet the visitors, not knowing who they were, although he had heard rumors that someone was coming to arrest him.

Seeing them must have stirred mixed feelings in him. One of the two was not only familiar to him but someone he would claim was a friend. When asked on the witness stand: "You and John A. Montgomery were friendly, were you not?" he answered, "Yes sir. He was my witness and was going to swear against Bill Pruitt [Pruett], the witness against me in that other case." Then he was asked, "You had no motive for killing John A. Montgomery?" and he replied, "No sir. He was a good friend of mine. I would as soon think of hurting one of these men [jurors] as quick as I would have him."

His response to Hugh's appearance was quite another kettle of fish (or shine). As noted earlier, Mathis still nurtured a grudge against the deputy marshal for having taken a pistol from him during an earlier arrest. Now Hugh Montgomery was standing in his yard with a warrant for his arrest. Mathis' grudge about that confiscated pistol may well have been the principal catalyst that precipitated the tragedy that night.

In any case, that would occur hours later. For the time being, Mathis pretended to be cordial. He would testify about first greeting the officers: "On November 16th Mr. Hugh Montgomery and Mr. John A. Montgomery come to my house about sundown and arrested me. Mr. Hugh read the indictment to me. I had just killed a hog and scalded it and was scraping the hair off. I asked him to stay until I got my hog cleaned. I told him I could go now but I would like for him to let me get my hog fixed up."

Mathis was lucky he had such a logical excuse. A hog was a valuable farm commodity, and this fall ritual produced an important staple food for a farm family during the following winter. According to Mathis' testimony, John A. Montgomery said, "Of course we will stay. It is just with Hugh about staying all night."

Hugh was more reluctant and said, "I ought to get back to town."

His companion offered, "I will stay here and you can go back."

At that point Hugh gave in, saying, "I ain't askeered to stay with Will."

During this exchange Mathis was already thinking ahead. Since neither of the Montgomerys knew who Lester was, he had a lie ready. As Mathis testified: "They asked me the negro's name and I told them Threlkill. Hugh asked if he was a brother of Bob and Frank Threlkill."

In her recount of the darkening hours of that Saturday, Cordie Mathis would second her husband's recollection. Only she would add a key point about Lester: "They come before sundown. Will was killing hogs. The negro was helping him. They hollered around at the front side and I told Will. He went around to the front and while he was around there the negro said to me, 'I am a good mind to kill them men.' I told him he wasn't going to do anything such, that I wasn't going to have any such as that."

In later legal proceedings, all the primary parties to the tragedy would be asked to give their versions of what happened. The third witness on the stand was one of the accused, Orlando Lester. Here is some of the exchange between him and District Attorney W. A. Roane:

> **Q.** State to the jury in as clear way as you can what happened after John A. Montgomery and Hugh Montgomery got to Will Mathis' on the evening of November 16, 1901.
> **A.** After they got there Mr. Mathis asked them to stay all night with him that night. He said he didn't care to come to town that night but wanted them to wait until morning to come to give him a chance to make bond without having to go to jail.
> **Q.** What did they say to that?

Lester recalled that John Montgomery said he didn't care: "It is with you, Hugh. It don't make no difference with me. The man has got his hog down here and is in bad shape to leave tonight."

Hugh replied, "I don't care. I will stay. I can go tomorrow night on the train."

Lester continued his testimony: "Then Mr. Mathis went on helping me clean the hog. After we got the hair off he holp me hang it up and he went in the house and made a fire and asked them in the house. He come out and told me about the time I got through cleaning the hog he wanted me to go off and get his gun."

Another witness at the Mathis trial was George Jackson, his friend, who spoke with Mathis before daybreak the following morning. The district attorney questioned him closely about what Mathis had related to him in that cold, dark meeting. After Jackson repeated much of what the others had said about waiting until the next day to go to Oxford, he added a new detail:

> **A.** [Mathis] said him and Hugh had a private talk and that he told Hugh about some kettles being there in that neighborhood.
> **Q.** What sort of kettles?
> **A.** Something they make whiskey in.
> **Q.** Go ahead now.
> **A.** He said he told Hugh that Mr. Jim Pilcher had a kettle and Frank Jackson and Hennel Sigler had up some beer but he didn't know whether they were at work or not.

In other words, Mathis was snitching on other moonshiners with the revenue agent. The presumption is that the families were rivals, since Mathis would tell Hugh later that night that Jim Pilcher had waylaid and threatened him. So Mathis could have regarded this as an opportunity to get at least Pilcher out of the way. Of course, by passing along information, he also could hope that Montgomery would regard him more leniently.

Jennifer Standifer was a correspondent for the *New Orleans Picayune* who came up to Oxford after learning of the sensational case. She was able to interview Mathis, and for this reason she appeared as a witness for the State. She testified as follows:

> **Q.** Have you ever seen Will Mathis?
> **A.** Yes, sir. I saw him in the county jail here in Oxford.
> **Q.** When?
> **A.** Saturday afternoon after the killing of the Montgomerys.

She was able to supply an additional piece of evidence, regarding Mathis' sobriety, when the officers showed up: "I asked him if he was drunk on the evening of the killing. He said he was pretty full of whiskey, that he had been drinking all the afternoon, but that he wasn't so full that he didn't know what he was doing and that he treated them right and got them to stay."

All the while Mathis knew that he was under suspicion of murder. That's why he had gone to Walter Jones and extorted the written statement that he did not believe that Mathis was connected with the murder of Hamp Williams. He had good reason to assume that the warrant for revenue violation was merely covering up the Montgomerys' real purpose: taking him into custody and then connecting him in some way with Williams' murder.

Mathis was not alone in his anxiety about the officers. His assistant at hog butchering had good cause to be nervous too. Mathis would relate later: "By this time Arlandus Lester had got the hair off of the hog, and we hung the hog up to dress it, Lester went to get a bucket of water to wash the hog down, but he never came back; he thought the officers wanted him, too, by me telling his name was Threlkeld [Threlkill], and he knew the talk was that he killed Williams, so he went to Whit Owens and told him that the officers were at my house and were going to stay all night."

Cordie Mathis remembered that Lester was fearful as well. On the witness stand, the following exchange took place:

> **Q.** Was the darkey afraid the officers had come after him?
> **A.** Yes, sir. They had called his name that night.
> **Q.** They had asked for him that night?
> **A.** Yes, sir. And he thought they were after him.
> **Q.** Did your husband tell the officers the darkey's right name?
> **A.** I don't know.

After Lester and Mathis had hung the hog, Mathis entered the house, according to Lester, made a fire, and invited Bill Jackson and the Montgomerys in. Then he came outside again. In court, Lester would describe what happened next: "He come out and told me about the time I got through cleaning the hog he wanted me to go off and get his gun." Asked where he was to go, he responded, "Down to Mr. Owens."

"Whit Owens?" the district attorney asked.

"Yes, sir. I asked him what he was going to do with it and he told me he would tell me about it after a while. So he went back in the house and come back out there again and told me what he wanted with the gun."

The prosecutor asked what he did want with it, and Lester answered, "He said he wanted to kill them fellows there and then. He told me to go and get George Mask's gun and tell Mr. Owens to come and bring his gun."

Lester walked to Whit Owens' house nearby and met the older man. Owens told him to go on up to George Mask's house, which was just north of the Owens place. Finding no one at home, Lester entered the house and took a double-barreled shotgun from a rack and went back to see Owens. The two talked briefly.

Owens asked if he had gotten the gun, and Lester said yes. Owens then said to tell Will Mathis that he could not come to his place because his wife had warned him that she would alarm the county if he did so.

Lester would later testify, when asked if he had shells for the gun, that he did not. Other testimony would argue that Whit Owens had supplied two shells full of buckshot. The general opinion was that Lester probably obtained both the murder weapon and the shells from Owens. The *Daily Clarion-Ledger* in Jackson would later report:

> It is positively known that Mathis sent to his father-in-law, Whit Owens, for a gun, but whether Orlando Lester secured the Owens gun or borrowed one without leave at the home of George Mask will never be known. The negro says he secured the gun at the home of George Mask.
>
> The negro admits that he went to the home of Owens and procured some shells for the gun, but he has perjured himself so many times on the witness stand that little reliance is placed in his statements, and the belief has always been that both the gun and shells were obtained from Owens, and that

the latter was informed by Lester at the time of what they intended to do.

When Lester returned, he found the group gathered inside for dinner. According to the trial transcript, Lester told what happened next:

Q. State to the jury what time you got back to Mr. Mathis' house.
No answer.
Q. Who?
A. Mr. Mathis and Bill Jackson and them two officers.
Q. So Bill Jackson was there when you got back?
A. Yes, sir.

By this time Cordie had finished trimming the hog entrails, and she came in and fixed supper for the men. According to most testimony, they ate around nine o'clock. John Montgomery sat at the head of the table, Hugh Montgomery sat to his right, and Bill Jackson sat to Hugh's right. Mathis was on John's left and held the baby, Clelon, in his lap while he fed him.

Mathis recalled the meal later:

> We all eat supper and enjoyed ourselves fine, John Montgomery and myself kept up a big laugh all the time, telling jokes; John told a heap of war tales and funny things that happened after the war.
> We got through supper. I carried them into the sitting room to the fire. I had been busy and didn't get in any wood; the fire was getting low; I told them to have seats that I would get some wood and make a better fire. I asked Hugh if he cared for me carrying my pistol out with me, told him that I had been waylaid by Jim Pilcher and his brother, that they had said they were going to kill me, and I always carried my pistol when I stepped out at night. Hugh said he would be like me and to carry my pistol on, he didn't care.

Part of the reason Hugh Montgomery was so lenient is

because, according to Cordie, Montgomery, Jackson, and Mathis had been drinking all evening. According to her, John Montgomery did not have anything to drink.

Mathis went into the kitchen and out the back door ostensibly to get wood. Though his version is self-serving, he told in his life story what he encountered once he ventured outside:

> As I stepped out in the yard I heard some one [sic] say "s-h-h," in a low whisper; I asked who it was; he said "s-h-h" again. I thought it was somebody trying to get to kill me; I thought there were two of them and it was one telling the other to shoot.
>
> I pulled my pistol and fired in the direction where I heard the whisper. After I shot I never heard anything more. I asked again who it was and never got any answer, I turned a bad dog loose I had tied to the tree I was behind and told him to "catch 'em"!
>
> The dog went right on to him; he threw his gun down and jumped up in a little sapling and called to me to stop my dog, and told me who he was; it was Lester; he said he had come to help me finish my hog. The officers ran to the door but found it was Lester and went back to the fire.
>
> When they went back Lester picked up his gun and told me that he had been there some time trying to get a chance to kill the officers, but some of my family was in the way all the time; he said he tried to kill them at the supper table, but could not shoot for me being in the way; he went on to state what Whit Owens told him to do as I have stated already. I told him he should not do it at all, that the officers were friends of mine and just doing their duty as officers; he kept begging me to let him kill them.
>
> My wife came out to where we were and Lester said to her, "Miss Cordie, oughtn't Mr. Will let me kill them, your pa said for me to do it; see, here is a hand full of buck-shot he gave me to kill them with; you know he keeps buck-shot all the time."
>
> My wife said, "I don't doubt pa sent you here to kill these men, but I will tell you right now, you are not going to hurt those men."
>
> I told him no, and for him to go and get some wood and chop it up and bring in and make a fire; he went and got the wood. Me and my wife went back in the house; she cleaned away

the supper table, and I went and sat down and commenced talking with John and Hugh Montgomery about a case I was to have in the Federal court. John Montgomery was a witness for me in that case.

Not surprisingly, Orlando Lester told a very different rendition of that conversation in the backyard. He pointed the finger at Will Mathis as the one who wanted to murder the law enforcement officers:

Q. When you got back with the gun, what did you do?
A. I stood around there and waited until he come out.
Q. What happened when you were standing around waiting?
A. Didn't anything only he come out and I called him and he snatched his pistol and shot.
Q. Did he shoot at you?
A. I don't know.
Q. What else was done?
A. He come out there and he said he just done that to get those men to come and there so he could kill them out there.

Yet when the Montgomerys merely looked out and then went back into the sitting room, Mathis told Lester to cut up some wood. Then Mathis took the gun and went inside the house.

Trying to pin the blame on Mathis caused the prosecutor at the trial to question Lester more closely about his motives.

Q. Were you and Will Mathis on good terms?
A. Yes, sir. I suppose so.
Q. What made the cut across the back of your coat?
A. Mr. Mathis cut it.
Q. What for?
A. Just because he wanted to, I reckon.
Q. Had you done anything?
A. No, sir.

Lester testified that he hadn't done anything to anger

Mathis that night. When pressed about whether he had ever lied to Mathis or been whipped or beaten by him, Lester repeatedly answered, "No, sir."

Lester also offered another account of the dog's reaction to him. Rather than chasing him up a tree, he said the dog ignored him:

> **Q.** What about his dog?
> **A.** He turned the dog loose.
> **Q.** What did you do then?
> **A.** I never done nothing.
> **Q.** Didn't you run?
> **A.** No, sir.
> **Q.** Did the dog get hold of you?
> **A.** No, sir.
> **Q.** Why not?
> **A.** The dog knowed I was there and never paid no attention to me.

This version makes more sense, because the dog would be very familiar with Lester. At least in this instance, Will Mathis seems to have let his imagination run free in order to make his story sound good.

Lester's story about what then happened to the gun he had brought back likewise contradicted Mathis':

> **Q.** Didn't you go up there snapping the gun?
> **A.** No, sir.
> **Q.** What did you do with the gun?
> **A.** I gave it to Mr. Mathis and he put it under the door steps.
> **Q.** Then what did you do?
> **A.** Cut up some wood and carried it in the house.

Yet lest anyone think Lester himself was being totally honest, the prosecutor's probing further into his motives produced a clear falsehood:

> **Q.** Had you done anything in that country to make you afraid of the officers?

A. No, sir.
Q. Hadn't you violated the law?
A. No, sir.
Q. You didn't think then that those officers came after you?
A. No, sir.
Q. Did Mr. Mathis tell you they came after you?
A. No, sir.

He then corroborated Mathis' testimony that Mathis had told the marshals his name was Threlkill. When pressed if Mathis had told Lester that the marshals were looking for him, Lester said, "No, sir." Questioning Lester's motives, then, the prosecutor followed up:

Q. What was your reason for taking part in this thing, going after the gun and coming back?
A. Mr. Mathis told me to.
Q. You would do anything he told you to at that time?
A. No, sir. I don't know that I would do anything.
Q. Did you refuse to do anything he told you?
A. I don't know.
Q. You don't remember anything that you refused to do?
A. I don't know, sir.
Q. What did he shoot his pistol for?
A. He tried to get them out of doors so as to kill them out there.
Q. How do you know?
A. That is what he said.
Q. When did he tell you that?
A. He told me that there that night.
Q. That was before you got back with the gun? You hadn't given him the gun?
A. No, sir.
Q. He had not spoken to you then, had he?
A. No, sir. He was trying to get the officers out, to wake them up and get them out of the house and kill them with a pistol. He was trying to get them out. They were not asleep.

The DA also asked Lester about his level of sobriety that evening:

Q. How much liquor had you drunk that night and day?
A. I don't know how much that day. I drank a pint that night.
Q. This old white whiskey, wasn't it?
A. Yes, sir.
Q. What time did you begin drinking that pint?
A. I had a bottle full when I left Mr. Mathis' to go after the gun.
Q. Was the bottle empty when you got back?
A. There was a swallow or two in it.
Q. Had you taken as many as a half dozen or a dozen drinks that day?
A. Yes, sir. I guess I had taken as many as a half dozen.
Q. Then you drank about a pint that day, or more?
A. I don't know, sir. I expect I might.
Q. And a pint that night, and that was a quart of whiskey you had taken.
A. Yes, sir. I guess so.
Q. Then you were pretty drunk, weren't you?
A. Yes, sir.

In another trial, Will Mathis would be asked about giving Lester the moonshine that night. His answer doesn't square with Lester's, perhaps because he didn't want the jury to think that Lester was too inebriated to be capable of carrying out the killings:

A. The negro had picked up the gun and Jackson left and the negro got the gun and was going off back to Mr. Owens', and he stopped and wanted some whiskey.
Q. You had whiskey which he carried off that night?
A. He didn't carry off any.
Q. Didn't he carry off a pint?
A. No, sir. When he came back, he had a half pint Mr. Owens gave him. He said Mr. Owens gave it to him. He had a half pint. He had it colored red, and I know Mr. Owens kept his whiskey red.
Q. What color was yours?
A. I did not color mine.
Q. Then the liquor Lester had was not white?

A. No, sir.
Q. Then Lester was mistaken about his liquor being white, if he said so?
A. Yes, sir. It was homemade whiskey but colored red.

What can be agreed upon is that once Lester brought in wood for the fire, he and Mathis went back out to take down the hog and cut it up. They carried it into the kitchen and spread it out on the table to cool until morning. By then it was ten o'clock, and Bill Jackson got up to leave. He promised that he would ask Taylor Moore, a bail bondsman, to come the next morning to Oxford and pay the bail bond for Mathis.

Perhaps caused by how much everyone had been drinking, Jackson's mule got loose, and Lester and Mathis helped him catch it. Lester made no mention in his testimony of the mule chase but did recall some things that happened behind the house: "[Jackson] come out to where I was at the pot and Mr. Mathis went back in the house and Mr. Jackson stood there and talked to me awhile and then Mr. Mathis come back out there and told us he had done got them fellows off to bed now. Him and Mr. Jackson went out to the lot then, I think, and Mr. Mathis told me to go out there and get a jug of his he wanted to get some whiskey for Mr. Jackson and I got the jug and he filled up the bottles for Mr. Jackson."

Q. Then what occurred?
A. After he filled up the bottles he didn't have no stoppers and he told me to go and get some stoppers for Mr. Jackson's bottles and I went and got them.
Q. What kind of stoppers?
A. Cob stoppers.
Q. Where did you go to get them?
A. In the side room.
Q. You went in there with what?
A. A lamp.
Q. How many lamps were there in the house?
A. Only one.

Mathis would add more to this account in his memoirs: "Lester told Jackson what he wanted to do and asked him if I oughtn't to let him do it; Bill Jackson said 'No,' and 'don't you let him do it, Will, for it will cause you trouble as long as you live if you do.' I said, 'No he shan't do anything of the kind.' Jackson got on his mule to leave." Again, Mathis was intent on pointing out how often Orlando Lester evinced a desire to kill the marshals.

Once Bill Jackson had left, only the four men were left: two criminals and two lawmen. While a friend, Jackson was also a potential witness. Whether or not Will Mathis or Orlando Lester pulled the trigger, neither would want anyone to tell others what happened next. The stage was set for the ultimate act.

Chapter Six
Pistol Claim Dispute

When Will Mathis came back into the house, he asked the Montgomerys if they were ready for bed. It had been a long day, and they were all tired. Mrs. Mathis had already retired to the main bedroom and placed Clelon in his crib. When the marshals answered in the affirmative, Mathis took the kerosene lamp and led them into the side room. (At various times this room was referred to as a shed room.) Exactly what happened there is related differently in conflicting accounts. In his life story, Mathis would relate the tale in this manner: "I carried the lamp into a back room and set down on the front railing to hold the light for them to go to bed. John Montgomery got in the bed at once; Hugh seemed to be slow in getting in the bed. Hugh Montgomery had a pistol of mine that he and McAdams, a U.S. detective, had taken from me in August, 1901, when they arrested me on the charge of passing bad money."

He recalled that they had put him in jail, and he had to stay a few days before the bail was paid. According to him, they gave the pistol to the jailer to hand over to Mathis when he departed, but Hugh Montgomery seized the pistol from the jailer the next day. When Mathis got out on bond, he asked the jailer for his pistol, and he said that Hugh Montgomery had taken it to the courthouse. He then pulled out a pistol that looked suspiciously like Mathis' and said, "I have one just like yours that cost me $14.50." Mathis went to the district attorney and asked him about his gun, and he said McAdams had taken it with him to Washington.

Mathis soon learned otherwise. He was told by a cousin

of Hugh Montgomery that Hugh had his pistol. Earlier on the afternoon of the 16th, before they went into the house, Mathis had asked Montgomery about it. Hugh said McAdams had it, even though he had no right to it. He promised that he would see about having it returned to Mathis.

"But as Hugh pulled off his clothes to go to bed I saw him pull off a shoulder scabbard with his coat with my pistol in it; he laid the coat and pistol under the pillow together; he pulled a pistol out of his pants pocket and threw it down and pulled off his pants, then placed the pistols under his pillow and got in bed; as he got in the bed I asked him to let me see the pistol he pulled off with his coat and seemed to be so particular with."

The suspicious tone in Mathis' voice made the revenue officer defensive.

"I will show it to you some other time."

Mathis insisted, though. "Let's see it now." He had seen the end of the handle and knew the pistol was his. He went on angrily, "You told me a damn lie about that pistol! You have got it and I want it!"

In response, Montgomery grabbed for the pistol and said, "God damn you, I will take you to town tonight!"

This heated argument between the two men brought Lester running, according to Mathis. He burst into the doorway with the shotgun raised. Lester, seeing Hugh armed, fired at the side of his head.

Once he stepped fully into the room, he found John A. Montgomery fumbling for his own firearm. Lester promptly fired the other barrel at him. "Neither of them spoke after they were shot," Mathis recalled.

At Mathis' trial, however, George Jackson gave an account that differs in one crucial aspect:

> **Q.** Tell what he [Mathis] said about the killing.
> **A.** He told me it was understood with him and the negro to kill those men and he said the negro was to do the shooting.

But he said when the time come for them to do the work he said the damn negro give down and that he had to do the shooting himself.

He said he shot Hugh Montgomery first right in the mouth, he thought, and that he had to shoot John A. Montgomery twice. He said the first time he shot him he didn't know for certain whether he hit him or not and that he shot him the second shot. And he said after he killed these men he taken his wife and little chap and they went down to Whit Owens' and that he told Mr. Owens what he had done and Mr. Owens said, "Did you do that sure enough?"

And what was Orlando Lester's statement? He ended up telling several versions: at the coroner's inquest, before the grand jury, as well as to various people with whom he spoke. He recounted a much different course of events. He stated that the twin killings had occurred earlier—before Bill Jackson left for the evening. He said the violence occurred when he went into the side room to get the corn cob stoppers for Jackson's moonshine jugs.

At the Mathis trial, District Attorney Roane questioned Lester closely:

> **Q.** How many lamps were there in the house?
> **A.** Only one.
> **Q.** Where did you go with that lamp?
> **A.** In the room where the officers were.
> **Q.** Where from?
> **A.** From the big room.
> **Q.** The living room?
> **A.** Yes, sir.
> **Q.** What occurred when you went in there with the lamp?
> **A.** [Mathis and Jackson] told them fellows they was after them. They says, "I come after you now. Give up. Raise your hands. If you don't, I am going to shoot you," and they didn't say nothing and didn't raise their hands and they shot them.
> **Q.** Who shot them?
> **A.** Mathis and Jackson.
> **Q.** Will Mathis and William Jackson?
> **A.** Yes, sir.

> **Q.** What did they shoot them with?
> **A.** Breech loader and Winchester.
> **Q.** Where were those men when they were shot?
> **A.** In the bed.
> **Q.** Were they dressed or undressed?
> **A.** Undressed.
> **Q.** Did they kill them or not?
> **A.** I suppose it killed them.
> **Q.** Did you see them afterward?
> **A.** Yes, sir.
> **Q.** Did they ever get out of the bed?
> **A.** No, sir.

Lester continued to maintain that he did not take a hand in the shooting, steadfastly declaring Bill Jackson and Will Mathis as the killers. Much later, though, when he was face to face with death, he would finally recant his accusation of Bill Jackson. By then Jackson was already in the Mississippi State Penitentiary serving a life sentence as an accomplice.

Mathis, on the other hand, claimed that Jackson was innocent, that he had left the Mathis place a little while before the shooting occurred.

The timing of the shooting was less in doubt. On the witness stand Ellen Welch was asked when she thought it happened:

> **Q.** How late did you stay up that night?
> **A.** Ten o'clock.
> **Q.** And the two shots occurred before you retired?
> **A.** Yes, sir.
> **Q.** About what time?
> **A.** Between nine and ten—nearer ten.
> **Q.** How many shots did you hear?
> **A.** Two.
> **Q.** Did both sound the same—one as loud as the other?
> **A.** Yes, sir.
> **Q.** How quick in succession were they?
> **A.** Tolerably quick.
> **Q.** Was there as much as a minute or two minutes between them?

A. There might have been.
Q. They were fired far enough apart for you to distinguish that there were two?
A. Yes, sir.
Q. Was it the sound of a pistol, shotgun or rifle?
A. I don't know——it was just a large sound.
Q. It didn't sound like a pistol, then?
A. No, sir. It wasn't a pistol.
Q. Did you get up and go to the door or window to see?
A. No, sir.

Coming back to the time of the shooting later in his examination of Ellen Welch, District Attorney Roane asked, "Did you hear any shots at all before you heard the two big guns?"

She said that she had not. Then he asked if she had heard more shots later on in the night, to which she replied, "Yes, sir. Two more large guns about the same size noise as the others." Asked if she had heard any other shots that night, she said, "Not until about 3 o'clock in the morning." Asked how many she had heard, she replied, "It seemed to me several pistols."

She would be the only person who could recall shots being fired three times that fatal Saturday night. The shooting in the dark at a suspected prowler and the shooting of the Montgomerys leave the third shooting she heard in question. Yet her testimony from trial to trial varied, a factor to consider when judging any witness's memory. At this trial, when asked if she had gone to the window or door to see what was happening, she said she had not. In a later trial, though, she would say that she and her husband had gotten out of bed at two o'clock. They had looked over at their neighbor's house but could see only a bed of coals. Back in bed, they discussed the light but dismissed it as the coals from the fire Mathis and Lester had built while cleaning the hog.

She admitted that she slept no more that night and was frightened, especially after the third shooting. The district attorney questioned her closely about the number and times of the shots:

> **Q.** Did you have a conversation with your husband about the light or guns?
> **A.** Yes, sir. We talked about the light.
> **Q.** What was said about it?
> **A.** I can't remember all that was said. I was frightened.
> **Q.** Why?
> **A.** I just couldn't sleep. I just got scared.
> **Q.** When did you become frightened?
> **A.** When I heard the guns.
> **Q.** The first guns?
> **A.** I wasn't frightened at the first guns. I had often heard guns there.
> **Q.** Was it any unusual thing for guns to be fired there?
> **A.** No, sir.
> **Q.** Why did you become frightened at the second guns?
> **A.** I don't know why it was, but I was frightened. I didn't know what time it was and was anxious to know what time it was.
> **Q.** Did you have any conversation with your husband about that light that you saw shining through the window?
> **A.** Yes, sir. We talked about it.
> **Q.** Did he get up then?
> **A.** No, sir. He didn't get up.
> **Q.** What did he say about it?
> **A.** He said, "Oh, Ellen, it is the moon shining. That is moonlight."

The sightlines to their other house, the one Will Mathis was occupying, were both near enough to know they were seeing something related to light, but far enough to obscure the true source. They were not seeing the coals from the hog butchering or the moonlight. It came from a deliberate attempt to obliterate all traces of a double homicide.

In the moments that immediately followed the murders, alarmed by the shots, Cordie Mathis rushed into the kitchen from the bedroom. In none of the testimony is any evidence that she saw the bodies of the lawmen at all. Will had her gather some things, and then the four of them—Cordie, Will, and Clelon Mathis and Orlando Lester—took the path down to Whit Owens' house. Before they left the murder scene, Lester asked Mathis to help him drag the bodies out to bury them. Mathis would later say:

> I told him to get the one that sent him, so my wife and I went down to her pa's; Lester went down there with us and called Mr. Owens up and told him that he had killed the officers and I wouldn't help him bury them and he would have to go and help him; Owens commenced putting on his clothes. When Owens started in the house to get ready to go to my house to help Lester with the dead men Lester gave him a lot of buckshot shells and said, "Here is your shells, I didn't have to use but two loads of them." Owens took the shells and the gun Lester had and carried them in the house and put them away. He got ready and we started back to my house. They asked me if I had a shovel; I told them I did not; Lester went up to Owens' lot and got one of Owens' shovels and carried it up to my house to bury the men with.

In this account, Mathis neatly excused himself from all wrongdoing, even to the point of refusing to bury the bodies because he had taken no part in the murders. At his father-in-law's third trial Mathis would give a slightly different version of the dark trip to Owens' home:

> **Q.** You went to Mr. Owens'?
> **A.** Yes, sir.
> **Q.** Where did you find him, if you found him at all?
> **A.** He was at his house. He had gone to bed.
> **Q.** Did you have a conversation with him or Lester, or together in your presence?
> **A.** I went in and told him to get up, that Lester wanted him to help bury those men, and Mr. Owens got up and went out to Lester and Lester handed him the gun and shells, and says, "I didn't have to use but two shells," and Owens says, "You made good shots, did you?" And he says, "Yes."

Q. State whether Mr. Owens made any statement to you at the house or going back about the matter?

A. While there at the house Lester asked if I had any shovel and I said "No." And he says "You had better get one," and he went up to his house or to Mr. Owens' lot and got one. He [Owens] said he told Lester to shoot the men and to tell me to alarm the country and tell the people came there and thought they were trying to kill me and made a mistake, and for him to go on back. He said he told Lester that, and said he would not have sent Lester if he had known those people were there and said he started to come himself, but Mrs. Owens began to cry and he sent Lester.

In this telling as well, Mathis laid another hint that Owens was the mastermind behind the whole affair. Almost to the moment of his death, he would suggest that he was merely a tool in someone else's hands, hinting broadly that it was Owens but refusing to name him, as if in doing so he would harm Cordie and Clelon. In his last few letters, as we shall see, he begged that his father-in-law not be allowed to raise his son.

The three men left Cordie and the boy with Martha Owens, Cordie's mother, and went back to Mathis' house. Details of the next hour or so also vary with the teller. The district attorney would interrogate Lester carefully about what unfolded at this point:

Q. When you got back up to Mathis' house, did you see those men?
A. Yes, sir.
Q. Where were they?
A. In the bed.
Q. What did you do then, all of you?
A. I didn't do anything. Mr. Mathis went and got their pistols out of the bed.
Q. How did he get them?
A. He went and turned the cover back and taken them out of the bed.
Q. Tell the jury the condition the bed was in?

A. I don't know. I never noticed particular.
Q. Did you see any blood?
A. Yes, sir.
Q. Where were those men shot?
A. I don't know. It looked to me like they was both shot in the head.
Q. Did you look for any wounds anywhere else on them?
A. No, sir.
Q. What was done with them?
A. Mr. Mathis drug them off on the floor into the other room.
Q. They were in the side room?
A. Yes, sir.
Q. When he pulled them off onto the floor, what did he do with them then?
A. He pulled the bed mattress off on them.
Q. Then what?
A. He bundled up some clothes there and told me and Mr. Owens to carry them back with us.
Q. Anything else?
A. Yes, sir. A feather mattress and some quilts.
Q. Did you carry anything else back? A gun or anything of the sort?
A. Yes, sir. I carried the Winchester.
Q. What did you do with George Mask's gun?
A. It was down at Mr. Owens'.
Q. You left it there after the shooting the first trip down there?
A. Yes, sir.
Q. When he got the bed clothing pulled off on the men, what did he then do?
A. He cut the straw mattress open with his knife and set it afire with the broom.
Q. Where did he get the fire?
A. Out of the fireplace.
Q. You mean he stuck the broom in the fireplace and then stuck it to the straw mattress?
A. Yes, sir.

Of course, Mathis would tell the story differently, mentioning in the process that had Lester not omitted telling Owens about Bill Jackson earlier, the whole affair might not have happened: "As we were going back to my house Owens found out that Bill Jackson had been to my house and had gone to get a bondman for me. Owens said that if Lester had told him that, he wouldn't have sent him to kill the men, and said he wished he had come on with Lester at the first like he started to do."

According to Mathis, when Owens and Lester reached Mathis' house, he started out to the back lot to catch his mule to leave. Owens asked him why he wasn't going to help bury the officers, and Mathis told him, "That isn't my job."

"Why not?"

"Because everybody in the county knows that those men were at my house. Before daybreak, there will be men here looking for them."

He further pointed out that it didn't matter where they buried the bodies. They would be found and the people who buried them would be tracked down with bloodhounds.

When Mathis went to the lot to catch his mule, though, he found it gone. Instead, he saddled Hugh Montgomery's horse and returned to the house. He went inside to get the pistol that Montgomery had withheld from him, and he met Owens coming out of the sitting room. He reported that he saw Lester putting a straw bed on top of them.

"I went back in the side room where the men were killed to get my pistol," he went on. "[I] found my pistol and two others and a pocketbook with $3.00 in it; I picked them all up and carried them off with me; that is all I carried away from the house."

Seeing that they intended to burn the house, Mathis went to his bedroom and from his bureau he fetched some clothes that belonged to their baby who had died. He gave them to Mr. Owens and told him to take care of them, and started out. Along the way, he claimed, "the negro picked up a chunk of fire and threw it over in the corner of the house. Mr. Owens said for him to wait awhile and made him put the fire back in the fireplace."

Again, Mathis had slanted the story in such a way that he

seemed like the aggrieved party in the proceedings. On the witness stand his responses to the prosecutor's questions about the disposition of the corpses directly contradicted Lester's version. In the following excerpt, the DA's increasing skepticism comes through clearly:

> **Q.** You are certain that Lester and Whit Owens had pulled the men off the bed?
> **A.** The two men were drug off the bed when I went in there to get my pistol. And I picked up the other pistols and the pocket book and put them in my pocket.
> **Q.** How much money was in the pocket book?
> **A.** Three or four dollars.
> **Q.** You got the money out of John Montgomery's pocket, didn't you?
> **A.** No, sir. I stated before the coroner's jury I did but I never.
> **Q.** Did you get Hugh Montgomery's knife?
> **A.** No, sir. I borrowed his knife that night before supper.
> **Q.** Did you get his cartridges out of his pocket?
> **A.** No, sir. I got them out of the belt. His belt was lying in the bed.
> **Q.** How about Hugh Montgomery's watch?
> **A.** I don't know a thing about that. It was took off after I left. I guess Mr. Owens or the negro got it. I never took anything but the three pistols and the money and the cartridges.
> **Q.** And the horse and bridle and saddle?
> **A.** Yes, sir.
> **Q.** And the rubber coat on the saddle?
> **A.** I don't remember that. If the coat was on the saddle, I got it.
> **Q.** Didn't you take that watch off and give it to Whit Owens?
> **A.** No, sir.
> **Q.** And didn't you tell him to take it and take care of it and if you never got back and your baby got old enough to know something about a watch give it to him?
> **A.** No, sir. I told them that before the coroner's jury but it isn't true.
> **Q.** Why did you tell that then?
> **A.** They asked me about the watch and I thought the best thing I could do was to tell something.
> **Q.** And you just told the first thing you thought of?

A. No, sir. I tried to think of what was the best thing to tell to save my life.

Q. And you thought the best thing was to tell them you took the dead man's watch off of his dead body and told your father-in-law to give it to your child when he got old enough to use it?

A. I didn't think that. I think you are mistaken about that.

The prosecutor's patent disbelief stemmed from the testimony of a third party, Bill Jackson. In his telling, Mathis was far more the director of the cremation than someone outside saddling Hugh Montgomery's horse:

Q. What did he say when he returned?

A. He said that he decided to burn the men up and that they had bled on the bed clothes and in the house and he decided he had better burn them up too. And he said he taken them by the heels and drug them off the bed onto the floor and put the straw mattress on top of them and then split the mattress open and stuck fire to it and shut the door and went out and left.

But the bodies were not only cremated. Mathis would later tell an *Oxford Globe* reporter: "Lester and I searched the bodies and effects of the dead men and took from Hugh a watch, two pistols, three or four dollars and a yellow coin about the size of a ten-dollar gold piece. From John we got 50 cents in money. I left Hugh's watch on a chair and think it burned up. I told them that if they never saw me again I wanted my baby to have the watch. Lester wanted to cut off the limbs and heads of the men, but Whit Owens said that would be too bad. I got a few things out of the house that I wanted to save, among them the clothes my wife had saved that our dead baby had worn, also a feather bed and some other things, which we carried down to Whit Owens'. The other feather bed was so full of blood that we had to burn it to keep it from giving us away. I then ripped open a straw bed, put the broom in the fire and set fire to the straw bed on top of the two men. Luster and I had dragged their bodies out in the hallway and the house was soon afire."

Though Owens may have objected when Lester suggested cutting off the arms and legs of the victims, the trio must have agreed to do it anyway, thinking that the corpses would burn faster if they were dismembered. The chore may not have been as brutal as it might seem, since both Mathis and Lester had been chopping apart a hog just the day before.

When Dr. P. W. Rowland, who performed the autopsies on the two marshals, came to the stand, he detailed the dismemberment:

> The trunk of the body was the only part left intact. The legs were off about half way between the knee and hip joint.
>
> The entire body was very much charred. The back of the skull was off. The lower jaw and part of the upper jaw was present with a few of the teeth. The arms were contracted in this fashion [drawn]. The fingers off and the spinal column thrown back.
>
> This bone here [arm] seemed to have been cut with a sharp instrument. There was a violent contraction of all the muscle remaining, especially the arms and abdomen.

In one of its stories about the crime, the *Globe* commented on the condition of the bodies: "The two bodies were burnt and battered into pieces, the top of their heads were burnt off, their legs, arms were burnt off, their bodies were burnt almost to a crisp—a ghastly sight. The jaw bones were all that was left of the heads, and it is very evident that after they were shot that their heads were battered by some hard instrument."

An indication of who did the butchering was given by Orlando Lester as he waited for the noose to be placed around his neck. In a brief dialogue with people standing around the gallows, Lester was asked: "Tell us if you cut the legs off the

Montgomerys the night of the killing." "No, I didn't cut their legs off. They wasn't cut off that I know of."

Two murders had occurred, and the house owned by Dan Welch was set on fire in order to hide all evidence of the crimes. Despite this panicked attempt to evade punishment, however, the fire would not incinerate the bodies fully enough by daybreak to remove all traces of the murdered men. With their ghastly remains in full view, the spool of events would be unraveled when the police descended on the remote hollow the next morning. Before the day was out, only Will Mathis would remain on the lam.

Chapter Seven
Posse Search

The rest of Saturday night would be cold, dark, and very busy for Will Mathis. At his father-in-law's suggestion, before he mounted Hugh Montgomery's horse, Mathis waited while John Montgomery's horse was saddled. He rode away leading John's horse behind him. After about two miles he turned the second horse loose, knowing someone would find it the next day. Mathis rode on to George Jackson's house, called for him to come out, and told him what had happened.

In that first report of the crime he laid the guilt all on Orlando Lester. His ostensible reason for seeking out Jackson was to make arrangements to prove that he had not been home the night Lester killed the officers. That was the alibi he had concocted and told his father-in-law before he rode off.

When District Attorney Roane questioned Jackson, he testified that he had been at his mother's house, where he lived, when Mathis rode up and yelled out to him.

    Q. What time?
    A. About an hour before day.
    Q. How come you to see him?
    A. He come to our house, and hollered at the gate.
    Q. Did you go out to him?
    A. I was sleeping in the back room and my youngest brother heard him and got up and went out and he asked was I at home and my brother told him yes.
    By the Court: Did you hear that?
    A. No, sir.
    Q. Did you get up and go out to Mathis?
    A. Yes, sir.
    Q. Tell what he said to you in that conversation.

A. When I got out there he spoke to me and I to him and I says, "Will, what the devil are you doing here this time of night." He sorter laughed a little and says, "George, I am in trouble." And I says, "What about?" He seemed he didn't want to tell me much and he says, "Can you do anything for me or will you?" And I says, "I always do all I can for a friend." I told him to tell me what was the matter. He seemed he didn't much want to tell me but he finally told me what had happened."

Among other things George Jackson said was the matter of who instigated the burning of the bodies. In this telling, Mathis was not a bystander: "He said that he decided to burn the men up and that they had bled on the bed clothes and in the house and he decided he had better burn them up too. And he said he taken them by the heels and drug them off the bed onto the floor and put the straw mattress on top of them and then split the mattress open and stuck fire to it and shut the door and went out and left."

When questioned about the horse Mathis was riding, Jackson said that Mathis identified it as Hugh Montgomery's. After they had talked a few minutes and Jackson understood the gravity of the situation, he got dressed and climbed onto the horse behind Mathis. They rode through the country to Curdie Hall's house and turned the horse loose. Hall was a cousin of Hugh Montgomery's and someone they knew would return the animal home later. From there the two walked through the dawn to Bill Jackson's house and called for him to come out.

Having just left Mathis late the night before, Bill Jackson might well have been surprised to see him at his doorstep in the early morning light. After telling about Lester killing the men, Mathis explained that he wanted to be able to prove that he himself was away from home when it happened. Bill Jackson agreed and said they had better talk to his brother-in-law, Ken Vines, and arrange an alibi that Mathis had spent the night there.

Furthermore, Bill Jackson agreed to swear that he had been at the Mathis place and that Mathis left the officers there about sundown, that Jackson himself had stayed to finish the hog butchering, that later he had found Ken Vines, George Jackson, Mathis, and some other boy who would swear Mathis had been with them since seven o'clock the previous night. This "boy" was never identified or brought to the witness stand.

George would recall that when they drew near Bill Jackson's place, Mathis went behind a store to wait until George fetched Bill to them:

> **Q.** Then where did you go?
> **A.** Over in Dogtown.
> **Q.** Did you all keep out of the way of people and the houses by going through the woods?
> **A.** We didn't go by nobody's house. We stayed out of the way as much as possible.
> **Q.** For how long?
> **A.** Plumb on till we got over to Vines'.
> **Q.** How long before he was arrested?
> **A.** That was Sunday. He was arrested on Wednesday.
> **Q.** How many days were you out with him?
> **A.** Plumb until Wednesday morning.

In considering these conversations Mathis had that Sunday morning, it should be noted that his audience knew nothing except what he told them. While he was scurrying about the Yocona community, laying the groundwork for an alibi, the alarm had yet to be sounded. Even his neighbors were not aware of the significance of the shots heard in the night or the glow on their bedroom walls later in the night.

"On Sunday morning, November 17, Dan Welch, a neighbor living close by, discovered my house was burned down," Will Mathis would write. Welch collected a neighboring family and went to the house to investigate. "[He] found the Montgomerys about burned up; he poured water on them and put them out and telephoned to Oxford for the officers to come; he thought it was Bill Jackson and myself that burned up; that a crowd of negroes had come and killed us and set the house on fire to take revenge from the shooting of Jones and Williams, but as soon as Montgomery's people got there they said it was John and Hugh Montgomery. Hugh Montgomery's brother knew him by a gold tooth; John Montgomery's son knew him by a small piece of his shirt that was lying under him that never burnt, and a pocket-knife he found that he recognized as his father's."

Ellen Welch, Dan Welch's wife and the neighbor who had been visited by the Montgomerys the previous afternoon, described the scene on the witness stand:

> **Q.** At daylight what did you discover next morning?
> **A.** I discovered that Will Mathis' house was burned down—it was our house but Will Mathis lived in it.
> [At one of the trials for Whit Owens, Ellen Welch would note that Mathis would have lived in the house exactly a year come December.]
> **Q.** Did you go over there that morning?
> **A.** Yes, sir.
> **Q.** Who went with you?
> **A.** My husband and family and Mr. Roebuck's family.
> **Q.** What did you find on getting over there?
> **A.** I found two persons burnt up.
> **Q.** Was Mrs. Roebuck with you?
> **A.** Yes, sir.
> **Q.** Had the house been entirely consumed or was it still burning?
> **A.** It was still burning but it was all burnt down and nothing left hardly, just fire coals.
> **Q.** Were the bodies burning?
> **A.** Yes, sir.
> **Q.** What did you do if anything toward rescuing the bodies?
> **A.** Mrs. Roebuck and myself wanted water poured on the bodies—and someone spoke up and said they thought it was against the law to go near the bodies—and I told them that I didn't think the law would hurt anybody to throw water on the bodies and put out the fire—and Mrs. Roebuck said yes she would do it

if they didn't, so my husband and Mr. Roebuck poured water on the bodies and put out the fire to stop them from burning.
    Q. Could you tell whether or not they were human bodies?
    A. Yes, sir. I think they were.
    Q. Did you see the bodies removed?
    A. Yes, sir.
    Q. Were there any clothes on either of the bodies?
    A. Yes, sir. There were clothes on them—I think they had on all their clothing but they were badly burnt.
    Q. Was there anything on top of them at all?
    A. There was straw on Mr. John A. Montgomery.
    Q. Was it entirely consumed or still burning?
    A. Still burning—just the ashes.
    Q. When you first got there could you tell there was but one body there?
    A. No, sir. Not hardly.
    Q. What did you do before you discovered the second one?
    A. Someone drew water and poured on Mr. John A. and I don't know who first discovered Mr. Hugh Montgomery.

A few minutes later District Attorney Roane came back to the question of the bodies:

    Q. You say you saw the bodies of Mr. John A. Montgomery and Mr. Hugh Montgomery in the ashes?
    A. Of course at the time we didn't know who it was but since everything has gone like it has, I believe it was them.
    Q. You saw no marks of identification on them?
    A. No, sir, but I believe it was them.
    Q. You just saw two human bodies?
    A. Yes, sir.

Ellen's husband, Dan Welch, did not testify in the early trials; but when he was finally called as a witness, he added some details to the depiction of that gruesome Sunday morning discovery. The exchange also adds further suspicion about Whit Owens' part in the affair:

    Q. Were you there before or after the bodies of the dead men were removed?

A. I was there before.
Q. Did you see Whit Owens that morning?
A. Yes, sir.
Q. Where did you first see him?
A. There at that place.
Q. How came him there?
A. We sent for him. . . . I asked him if he thought it was Mr. Mathis and his wife, and he said no, his wife was at his house. I asked him if he thought it was Orlanda Lester and Will and he said it wasn't, that Orlanda was at home, and Will had went over to Bill Jackson's to stay all night.
Q. Did he say anything about when Mrs. Mathis went to his house?
A. He said she came down there after dark, and I told him I heard she was there at eight o'clock, and he said the darky brought her there sometime that night.
Q. Were you present when the two bodies were removed?
A. Yes, sir.
Q. What was done with the two bodies?
A. They were laid out in the yard there a little piece.
Q. What was afterwards done with them?
A. They taken them to my house the next night, on Sunday.
Q. Then what?
A. A crowd came from Pontotoc after Hugh Montgomery.
Q. Where did they carry him?
A. To Pontotoc, I suppose.
Q. What did they do with John Montgomery's body?
A. I brought him to Oxford myself.

One other person who spoke with Whit Owens that fateful Sunday morning—C. E. Slough, clerk of the circuit court—was called by the defense at an Owens trial and had this exchange with District Attorney Roane in cross-examination:

Q. Tell the jury what he [Owens] said about Mrs. Mathis?
A. He said that Mrs. Mathis and the little boy and Orlanda Lester came to his house about sundown the evening before, or dark, and that Will Mathis had gone to Dutch Bend.
Q. Did he say when Will went off?
A. Yes, sir. I asked him repeatedly if he had any idea and he said he did not.

Q. I will ask you if you didn't ask him about Will Mathis' gun, his Winchester?
A. Yes, sir. I asked him if he didn't think that was Will someone had murdered, and he said "No." And I asked him where was Will's gun and he said it was at his home and had been there for two weeks, I believe was his remark.
Q. Did he tell you how it happened to be up there?
A. Yes, sir. He told me why. He said where he lived there were a skirt of timber on the other side of his house and had been some large hawks there and he got the Winchester to kill the hawks, that a shotgun wouldn't reach them.
Q. And that it was there then?
A. He said it was at his home then. That was on Sunday morning and had been there two weeks.
Q. Now, didn't you question him pretty closely to know if he had any idea who those men were?
A. Yes, sir. I was very much concerned, and asked him repeatedly to try to get him to answer about it.
Q. Did he deny all the way through that he knew anything about it?
A. Didn't know anything about it.
Q. How far did you ride with him?
A. He rode with me from the burning to his house, nearly two miles towards Oxford, in the buggy with me.
Q. Did he ever say anything about the Montgomerys being there the evening before?
A. No, sir.
Q. Did you know then that the Montgomerys had been out there?
A. No, sir. I did not.
Q. What was his appearance? How did he look?
A. He looked like a man that was bothered very much over something.
Objected to by defendant and sustained.

A telephone message to the sheriff from Delay, received at eight o'clock Sunday morning, stated that a horrible crime had been committed the night before. At about 9:30 a horseman, Henry Thompson, rode swiftly into town. He was an African American who operated a sawmill owned by Tom Harkins, a brother of the sheriff's, so that's where he first went with his startling news. About all anyone knew at the moment was that pistol shots had been heard in the direction of the Mathis house at frequent intervals through the night. Around four o'clock that morning Dan Welch had seen smoke and flames against the sky, and when he and a neighbor, Lonnie Roebuck, investigated at daybreak, they had found Will Mathis' house burned nearly to the ground and the charred remains of the two officers in the ashes of the smoldering ruins. Such was the report brought by the workman.

Seventy years later, Marvel Ramey Sisk, Pete Ramey's daughter (who was four years old in 1901), would recount the next hours as they were told to her later:

> Quickly Tom Harkins saddled his white horse, Selim, and together the two men rode hurriedly to the home of the sheriff. John Harkins had been quite ill for several days and was still confined to his bed. All he could do was to send for his deputy and give a few instructions; so the responsibility for the manhunt which followed fell upon the shoulders of the young deputy, Pete Ramey, who went directly to the sheriff's office to set the wheels of the law in motion.
>
> News of the tragedy spread rapidly. Saddle horses appeared at the iron hitching posts around the courthouse, normally unused on Sundays. Grim-faced men gathered in small groups in the sheriff's office and in the corridor outside, talking in low, shocked tones of the crime, and ready to do what they could to help apprehend the criminals.
>
> A posse had been organized to leave almost immediately. Several men had been deputized to make arrests and organize other posses that would join the first as necessary. After attending to many other such details Pete Ramey prepared to leave with the first posse. He had ridden his horse when he went to talk over the situation with Sheriff John Harkins earlier that morning. Now he rode home to give his horse a good feeding and to grab a bite to eat himself before leaving, wondering when either would have a good meal again, as they would have to depend on what food they could get at scattered farmhouses, if they were lucky enough to pass one. When he

[Pete Ramey] told his wife goodby [sic] he said that he would come home as soon as possible, but that he would not return until the killers were caught.

    J. F. Matthews, the office deputy US marshal, set in motion the manhunt that would find the killer or killers and bring them to Oxford to face trial. He and his posse rode out of Oxford around eleven o'clock, but not until nearly two o'clock that afternoon did G. R. Hill, clerk of the US Court at Oxford, telephone Marshal Buchanan in Holly Springs about the murders. Buchanan immediately authorized Hill to spread the word that Buchanan was offering a $100 reward on his own for information leading to the culprits' capture. He also telegraphed Washington, asking for permission to hire A. Z. T. Johnson, a former deputy marshal, as a special detective on the case. Johnson knew the vicinity and as deputy marshal had on former occasions performed "most valuable and difficult services in this same neighborhood."

    A posse of two dozen men and officers found upon arriving at the scene that without doubt the bodies were those of the two officers. It was supposed on the scene that after making the arrest, the Montgomerys had been induced to await daylight to return, and that friends of Mathis' assisted in overpowering and murdering them, then setting fire to the house and escaping.

    The search was on. The fact that such a terrible crime could be perpetrated upon officers of the law was an added incentive to everyone gathered there to find the desperate moonshiner Mathis, who had proven he would stop at nothing in his sordid career in crime. That, all of them were determined, was plenty enough reason to hunt him down like a dog.

Chapter Eight
Mathis Eludes the Lawmen

The men who were trying to capture Will Mathis suffered from a distinct disadvantage: none of them knew the swamp-filled bottomland as well as he did. He had lived there, after all, for five years. In addition, he had been forced to go into hiding before. While the severity of the crimes he had committed was now of a significantly larger magnitude, his moonshiner's knowledge of how to evade capture had been honed numerous times.

Those who lived nearby were not afraid only of Will Mathis, though. That Sunday the entire county had to fear all of the outlaws, none of whom was yet in custody. According to Marvel Ramey Sisk:

> Fear had spread throughout all the rural communities of the Yocona area. Unwilling to stay alone, Dean Jones and her little daughter, Rosa, went to spend the night with Lela Murray and her three children, Nina, Euphus, and Mildred. Ben Murray returned rather late that night to get a fresh horse.
>
> Through a window he saw that his family was all right and that they had company, so Nov. 17, without making his presence known, he quickly changed horses and returned to his post. The next morning Nina Murray had occasion to go to the barn. She saw the horse her father had ridden when he left home, and came running breathlessly back to the house, feeling sure that something had happened to her father. Later, they missed the horse which had been taken in exchange, and realized what had happened, but not before the family had been thrown into a panic.

At one point Mathis was close enough to hear his hunters talking. Ben Murray and Buddy Jones, neighbors in the Yellow Leaf community, had joined one of the three posses put together after the hunt began. They took up a guard post at Cantrell Bridge, since it was thought that Will Mathis might try to escape that way. Mathis was hiding under the edge of the bridge among some large roots of a tree that grew on the bank. He saw Murray and Jones, as well as Dick Oliver and Tom Ragland, and said later he could easily have killed them.

In his dictated life story, Mathis would amplify this point:

> On Sunday evening, November 17th, George Jackson and I went to Whit Owens', got there about dark. I intended to come on to Oxford and give up; Whit Owens said for me not to do it, that they would mob me as soon as they found me; that everybody believed I killed the men and burned them, and it wouldn't do for me to give up at all; he said for me to fight till I died, not give up at all for they would mob me, and get as many of them as I could; Owens said, "I have got your Winchester in the house, do you want it?" I told him yes; he had the gun brought to me, and Jackson and I went back to Dutch Bend, close to Jackson's house, and slept in a cotton house that night.

In his testimony at his trial, he would be asked about the rifle:

> **Q.** You had a lot of Winchester cartridges?
> **A.** Yes, sir. I wasn't going to kill anybody but to keep the move off of me. I could have killed the men several times if I wanted to.
> **Q.** Why didn't you tell the truth, that the negro did the killing?
> **A.** I didn't want to get Mr. Owens in trouble, and I knew he would give Mr. Owens away.

Since the onset of the search was quite disorganized, it is likely that Mathis did not boast amiss that he could have escaped completely had he wanted to. "I could have gotten out of the country without any trouble if I hadn't stayed around to see what became of my family," he said later. "It would have been the easiest thing in the world for me to have ridden right on through the country instead of riding into Dallas and surrendering if I had had a mind to." As it was, the entire area he hid in was no more than fourteen square miles, although reports of his being spotted much farther away came in.

Thinking that Mathis would probably come to his father-in-law's house to find out whether Owens and Cordie had returned from the inquest at Oxford—and then to sleep—the posse circled the premises and waited. With the first gray peep of dawn the word was given to close in. The posses approached the house, entered, and searched, but found nothing.

Shortly before dawn they heard two gunshots near the ruins of the Mathis house. They were now convinced that it was a signal from the fugitive, and that when he received no answer, he dived once more into the swamps.

Early Monday morning Cordie Mathis was brought in, along with her father, Whit Owens. Though they were put through a rigid examination by the coroner's jury, which was still sitting, they maintained they knew nothing of the crime. Despite their protestations, the jury ordered them to jail.

Orlando Lester had already been captured not far from the crime scene. Once Bill and George Jackson were taken into custody by mid-week, the entire gang—as the people of the community called it—would be rounded up. Friends of Mathis, such as Shell Vines and others who gave him food and refuge during his flight, were never charged with any crime.

On Monday, a report came from fifty miles southeast of Oxford:

> Okolona, Nov. 18.—(Special.)—Will Mathis, the supposed murderer of Deputy United States Marshals Hugh and John Montgomery, was seen at 12 o'clock last night in company

with his father at the house of his aunt, about five miles west of this place. After staying a short while they mounted their horses and left, going west in the direction of Schooner valley, where relatives reside. Mathis was born and reared in this county about twelve miles west of this place. His capture is almost certain.

The next day, Tuesday, it rained and nothing much could be done, although an attentive lookout was kept and all the avenues of escape from the neighborhood were protected in some way. That night the search was continued without result.

The only excitement that day came from Dave Rogers, the revenue officer who had had several run-ins with Will Mathis and whom on one occasion Mathis had tried to kill. Rogers received a threatening letter dated at Delay and mailed in Oxford that added more fuel to the inflamed rumors:

> Delay, Miss., Nov. 18, 1901.
> Dave Rogers:
> We wright you this to let you no your time is next, an aneybody else that come out here fooling about with our business. [Sentence omitted by all newspapers as being too vile to print.] This is to tell you your life is in your hans.
> This Is Us.

It seems unlikely that this was penned by Will Mathis. He was too busy trying to save his skin. In his autobiography he described his movements during those two days:

> On Monday morning George Jackson went home to get our breakfast; when he got back to where I was he told me that the officers got Bill Jackson the evening before and carried him to Oxford jail. We ate our breakfast and then went down in Yocona bottom and stayed in a cotton house that day and night, for it was a wet day.
> Tuesday night I heard that the officers were looking for me that day, and that they had sent for a pack of bloodhounds.

That news was correct. As the hunt for Will Mathis by

men on horses began to prove dwindling results, the federal marshals made the decision to bring in dogs. The first pack ordered were from out of the state. Bloodhounds from Water Valley, Tennessee, and Milan, Tennessee, were put on railroad cars headed south.

In addition, a second posse had been sent out on Monday to join the first, and a third one on Tuesday morning, until a hundred and fifty men surrounded the swamp where Will Mathis was supposed to be hiding.

On December 6, George M. Buchanan in the Marshal's Office in Oxford would write to the attorney general in Washington, DC, to explain why he had paid for the extraordinary request of dog trackers. The letter included this reasoning:

> It must be understood that Mathis undertook to avoid capture by concealing himself in a dense swamp of thousands of acres in Yocony [sic] river bottom, a wilderness of cane and small low under-growth, impenetrable except by means of narrow foot path-ways or trails, but familiar to Mathis who had lived in the neighborhood for many years. It was under these circumstances that a posse of from 50 to 100 mounted men [the word "volunteers" was written in above line] could do but little else than guard all points of egress from the swamp, until Mathis (armed with 3 pistols and Winchester rifle) might surrender from exhaustion and hunger, if he failed to escape. . . .
>
> I should not have obtained the services of these dogs without first consulting the Department, except for the fact that there was a pressing requirement for their presence with all possible haste, they having been brought from Milan, Tenn (on my telegram). . . .

The dogs from Tennessee arrived in Holly Springs, and Marshal Buchanan joined them for the trip south to Oxford, claiming later that he was in fact barely able to walk. The dogs went on out to the scene of the crime, but the marshal remained in his office in town.

On Wednesday, November 20, the special correspondent to the *Commercial Appeal* in Memphis would report:

Early this morning a pack of bloodhounds, in charge of Bobby Murray of Water Valley, arrived in Oxford and proceeded immediately to the scene of the crime. A trail was soon struck, and after devious wanderings the dogs bayed at the home of George Jackson, a bosom friend of Mathis, and a man believed to be with Mathis in his flight. Jackson was located in the house and placed under arrest. Then pressure was brought to bear on him to lead to his disclosing the whereabouts of Mathis. Not until certain death stared him in the face did he consent to lead the way to where he had spent the night with the fugitive from outraged justice.

The dogs took Mathis' trail at that point and followed it in a manner indicating its warmth until they found where Mathis had stolen a mule from the barn of the Price place. Here the officers were informed that the mule had thrown Mathis immediately after his mounting, and that Mathis had proceeded to another house nearby and procured a horse in the same manner as before, by appropriation.

Continuing his flight with the deep baying of bloodhounds ringing in his ears, the unhappy wretch came near riding into a wing of the posse which had circled his position. So hot was the pursuit that Mathis had to leave his horse for the third time.

Here, owing to some unknown reason, the bloodhounds refused the trail, which led into an almost impenetrable swamp known as "Kettle Bottom."

It is believed that, reverting to the methods adopted by fugitive slaves before the war, the hard-pressed fugitive had applied cayenne pepper to his shoes, thereby causing the well-trained dogs to lose the scent of man in the more pungent odor of this sneeze-producing agency. However this may be, the dogs could not again strike the trail, but the sixty determined men proceeded to stake out the ground and prepare for beating the bush in true tiger-hunting manner.

Crowded from pillow to post in broad fields of dense thicket, the inevitable was forced to the heated brain of Mathis, and he planned how a few more moments of life could be gained.

In point of fact, Mathis threw the hounds off his trail with an old Indian trick. When the dogs got close, he would tie bags of ground pepper to his ankles, and the pepper dusted out as he ran, foiling the dogs' sense of smell.

Despite this report, wild rumors as to Will Mathis' whereabouts continued to flourish. For instance, later on the same day the *Commercial Appeal* would report:

> Water Valley, Miss., Nov. 20.—(Special.)—City Marshal Rayburn tonight received a telephone message from Banner, twenty miles in the interior from this city, stating that Will Mathis, the supposed murderer of Deputy United States Marshals Montgomery, had just arrived there on a badly jaded horse, which he had abandoned, and stealing a fresh mount had started in the direction of Water Valley. Thirty minutes after he left Banner a posse of 150 mounted men, with bloodhounds, arrived, and taking up the trail left in hot haste after the fugitive. R. S. Murray, with his two bloodhounds, left here last night for Oxford to enter the chase, and it is supposed to be he and his dogs that are leading the posse. Murray has something more than a State reputation as a man hunter, and if it is true that he is only an hour behind Mathis he is about sure to bag him.
>
> Mathis is well known in this city [Memphis]. He has visited here for many years, and occasionally made this city his trading point. Your correspondent is reliably informed tonight that he is an own cousin of the famous bandit Rube Burrows, and when that desperado passed through this section, a year before his sensational death, he is reported to have visited Mathis and remained several days in seclusion about the place.

With so many men carrying weapons and prowling the rough countryside in pursuit of the fugitive, it is a little wonder that an innocent man did not get shot. The only fatality among the posses occurred not to a man but a horse belonging to Tom Ragland, the county jailer. The *Oxford Eagle* would later say this about Ragland's noble sacrifice: "Mr. Tom Ragland, of our town, joined in the hunt, and gave several days to the work without hope or expectation of remuneration. While engaged in the search Mr. Ragland's horse (a valuable one) was accidentally shot and killed, causing him serious loss. He has a large family dependent on him, and we believe it would be but just for the citizens of our town and county to compensate Mr. Ragland for his loss."

Mathis had nothing to do with the shooting, as Marvel Ramey Sisk explained: "Dick Oliver's gun had gone off by accident and had killed Tom Ragland's horse. The two men rode double into town to get another horse, then returned to pick up the saddle and join the hunt again. Mathis had been going through fields pulling up raw turnips to eat, and Dick Oliver and Tom Ragland had tracked him. It was then he decided to surrender."

Since Mathis had the ability to escape the area, the question naturally follows: Why didn't he? Through all of his furtive movements around the area, Mathis was constantly worried about what was happening to Cordie. The posse had expressly circulated the report that his wife was sure to hang unless he returned to save her. He wrote about his constant worry: "On Wednesday night George Jackson and I stayed at John Steward's; Steward told me that they had put my wife in jail, and that the negro Lester had told enough on her to break her neck, so on Thursday morning I told George Jackson I couldn't believe that my wife was in jail but I was going down to Whit Owens and see what I could hear, and if it was so about her being in jail I was going to her and do all I could to get her out of jail."

He daringly ventured back home to Whit Owens' "and ran right into a crowd looking for me; they were in 200 yards of me, and they saw me." As he fled across the Yocona bottomland, the dogs were put sniffing on his trail. "I went into Lancaster's [a neighbor of Owens] field, where he was at work, and asked him if he knew anything about my wife being in jail; he said she was, and the negro had told enough to hang her, and for me to swap out with the officers when they came on me, for they came to kill and burn me." Mathis told him that he intended to do just that before long. After all, the posse was after him with bloodhounds. He decided that he had to persuade the law to let his wife loose. "I went right back across Yocona bottom and got a horse from Ed

Wiley; I rode it a piece, turned it loose and got another horse, rode it about a half mile, got off of it onto another horse and never touched the ground. Right there I fooled the dogs and got away from them."

That same Wednesday the posse was joined by a large crowd that had ridden through from Pontotoc, Hugh Montgomery's home, and the search was resumed with redoubled energy. Two sets of bloodhounds were employed. George Jackson, who was known to have been with Mathis in the swamp for the past two nights, was caught and threatened that if he didn't tell where the fugitive was, he would be killed.

He took the former alternative without hesitation and led the posse to a spot in the swamp where the two men had spent the previous night. The place abounded with evidence that Jackson was acting in good faith. Behind an immense log were embers that showed where a recent fire had burned, and the ground was imprinted with fresh tracks. Jackson then accompanied the posse in their search, after first exacting a promise that the officers would protect him and not give Mathis an opportunity to kill him from ambush, proof of the fear inspired by Mathis in his associates.

Then followed hours of hot pursuit, through almost impassable cane thickets, mud, and sloughs, with fits of hope and dejection. When Mathis appeared at Hartfields, which was a telephone station, Miss Clyde Hartfield telephoned offices on the line. The searchers were at once notified and put on the trail. A special to the *Commercial Appeal* described the anxiety the posse members felt as they went deeper and deeper into dangerous terrain.

> It was not expected that he would be taken without a struggle which would result fatally on both sides. They knew that Mathis knew that there were men in some of the searching parties who were in favor of shooting or burning him on sight; and that the criminal was thoroughly impregnated with the very reasonable idea that surrender meant immediate death

or subsequent burning at the hands of a mob. The deputies and members of the posse knew, furthermore, that Mathis was reputed to be one of the best shots, both with pistol and Winchester, to be found anywhere. They were familiar with the stories of his remarkable skill that were current not only among the community but the officers who had had to do with him in the past, and had learned something of the desperate man.

With such a quarry, liable to turn at bay at any moment, and from some secret cover, deal death when he found himself trapped, every blundering step through the swamp was fraught with danger. Trying to follow his track by means of bloodhounds, missing it every now and then and searching far and wide to discover it again, confused by other tracks through the swamp, they did not know at what moment a leaden messenger from behind a tree or fallen log might show that the quarry had turned at bay, showed its teeth and had devoted himself to death and vengeance. These circumstances lent a piquancy to the pursuit that none of them were particularly anxious to enjoy again, unless, of course, it should prove to be necessary.

The man they were seeking did not know whether to sell out or give up. By "selling out" he meant kill as many of the posse as he could before they killed him. He had shared this idea with Owens earlier, and his sage father-in-law had opined that it might be the best choice. Shooting it out would, of course, have silenced a witness against the older man. Owens would try at a later time to silence his cohorts before they could appear on a witness stand.

On that Wednesday Mathis first went to the home of a cousin of Clyde Hartfield's husband, Curt Hartfield, which was on the south side of the Yocona River, twelve miles south of Toccopola, Mississippi. There he tried to hire the negroes on the place to take Hartfield's horses and pilot him to a friend's house on Patlaccana Creek. The negroes were badly frightened and ran to Hartfield's house and reported him. This caused Mathis to believe that a mob was after him, and he rode on to Dallas.

There the end of the four-day manhunt came quietly, without a single shot being fired. The desperado, with bloodhounds and an armed body of one hundred and fifty tired, but determined, men close on his trail, walked into L. A. Latham's store in Dallas about eight o'clock Wednesday night, laid his Winchester and three pistols down on the counter, and surrendered himself to Squire Oren Brown, Louis Latham, and John Phillips, to seek protection of the law.

On the witness stand, Mathis would recall those tense moments: "When I gave up at Dallas, Pete Ramey told me they were talking about mobbing my wife, and I says, 'Pete, ain't you going to protect me?' And he says, 'I will do what I can, but I can't fight for you.' And I came to town and saw the crowd and I didn't believe I could get to the jail house, and I

Will Mathis in jail

thought the crowd would take and mob her, and I decided to take the whole thing on myself."

Toward evening the posses received a telephone message at Denmark, a post office in the vicinity, that Mathis had surrendered. When the news reached Oxford there was great rejoicing, and bonfires were started in the shadow of the jail. Cordie Mathis, standing at the window of her cell, saw the flames and thought the fire was intended for her husband, that he might suffer the same fate he had inflicted upon his victims. Her screams of anguish could be heard for blocks. Those gathered around the jail heard her fervent prayer: "O Lord, I can not [sic] bear any more." Some time was required to allay her fears that the fires were meant only as jubilation, not retribution.

Orlando Lester in jail

The men who had taken part in the three large posses arrived home utterly exhausted. Often without food and sleep, they had sat in their saddles or stood in the rain hour after weary, watchful hour—some of them since Sunday. So it was a great relief when Will Mathis gave himself up. But they would have little time to rest for another long day and night. The little town of Oxford would pass through one of the most trying ordeals that ever perplexed an enlightened civilization—the threatened lynching of the two murderers. Every law enforcement officer and many levelheaded citizens would be needed to keep the threat from becoming a grim reality.

Chapter Nine
An Arrest and Its Uproar

Unlike the lawless wilds of the countryside, Oxford had earned a reputation as the decorous seat of the state's university. One in seven homes had a bathtub; one in thirteen had a telephone. They could bake cakes with sugar that cost four cents a pound. They had moved beyond owning cows and chickens, but they could purchase eggs for fourteen cents a dozen and butter for twenty-four cents a pound. Electricity was becoming standard, and automobiles on their thin, wood-spoked wheels were making their first appearance on the streets.

The town was connected to the trends of the modern nation. As Faulkner biographer Joseph Blotner would write: "A little over a half-mile west of the Square the trains of the Illinois Central would signal their stops at the depot with distinctive whistles. Just across the railroad tracks, a mile west of the Courthouse, lay the campus of the University of Mississippi, with its scattering of Greek Revival and Georgian buildings, set among magnolias, dogwoods, and redbud, as well as the tall shade trees on a square mile of elevated rolling land."

In an advertisement a local company Buffaloe & Buttler announced proudly, "We have now opened up our Ice Cream parlors and Soda Water for the season . . . and will say that our long experience in the business warrants us in saying that we can serve you with as nice and delicious soda water, and ice cream as can possibly be made, and would respectfully ask you to give us a call."

A. V. Hiler, who operated the only barber shop in Oxford at the time of the murders, ran an advertisement under the heading "NOTICE!" He said, "As I have employed experienced men by the month and have nothing else for them to do but to cut hair and shave, I will give the public the benefit of this day, by reducing the price of Shampooing, Shaving, Shining, &c, beginning next Monday. Hair Cut, 25¢ Shampoo, 15¢ Shave, 10¢, Shine, 5¢."

This was a respectable and respectful community where a stirring lecture might be expected. "All the stores agreed to close up town . . . and attend the decoration of the soldiers' graves at the Soldiers' Cemetery just west of the base ball [sic] grounds. The . . . Hon. J. E. Holmes will address the assemblage at the Soldiers' graveyard to-morrow evening. We anticipate an enjoyable address from this gifted young orator."

That such a horrible crime as the murder and cremation of two federal marshals had taken place in their county angered every citizen. Despite their polite behavior in quiet times, Oxford was still part of the South in an era when armed bands of citizens enacted justice at a fever pitch. Even before the capture of Will Mathis, US Marshal George M. Buchanan, from his sickbed in Holly Springs, had anticipated trouble related to protecting the fugitive. He wrote to his boss in Washington:

> The Excitement consequent upon the killing of Deputy Montgomery and guard Jno. A. Montgomery is likely to be renewed to a very Considerable Extent, whenever the trial of "Mathis" and his CoConspirators is held.
> And should the trial of these men be had in our Federal Court (to be held in the City beginning Monday next) the Marshal desires to be supported by such force as may be necessary to protect the prisoners and to support the court in the lawful disposition of these men. I therefore suggest that the Marshal be authorized to Employ a guard of not exceeding 25 men for the purpose stated, should such employment be deemed as best and proper thing to do for the occasion. It is the belief of the Marshal that he can select a force within the limitation as stated, of good men, who under the immediate authority and direction of the Marshal will be sufficient to deter (and if necessary to resist) any violence that may be attempted.

If Will Mathis feared the crowd of one hundred and fifty men that rode slowly back to Oxford with him, he had good cause to do so. In many parts of post-Civil War America the cherished Anglo-Saxon notion of the *posse comitatus* was very much alive and observed quite openly.

As in so many instances during the Will Mathis case, the Memphis *Commercial Appeal* vividly captured the unfolding scene:

> Oxford, Miss., Nov. 21.—(Special.)—Today at 11 o'clock the streets of Oxford presented an entirely new and unusual appearance. Since 8 o'clock last night expectations had been keyed to the highest pitch in anticipation of the coming of the notorious murderer, Will Mathis. There were many who doubted the ability of the officers to protect the prisoner on the journey from Dallas to this place, but at the appointed hour the advance guard of the posse hove into sight, and South street, through which they entered Oxford, was transformed into a military procession ground.
>
> Men with two days' growth of beard, smoke and dust-begrimed from constant duty either at the lonely camp signal fire or sleep astride their faithful steeds, armed with repeating rifles and shotguns of all descriptions, composed this hastily organized military company. The horses held their heads low and looked lank and lean from hard usage in the chase. A pack of bloodhounds, held in check by lead ropes, accompanied the procession and in its midst there rode a handcuffed and manacled prisoner at whose awful deed the civilized world has stood aghast.
>
> A man of less than ordinary stature, possessing no outward appearance distinguishing him from his fellow man, in the very prime of what should have been a happy life, Will Mathis was completing what he said was his last trip to Oxford.
>
> A great crowd was collected at the Lafayette county jail and as soon as it became evident that the courthouse and not the jail was the posse's destination, a wild scramble ensued. Men and boys raced for a position of vantage, where they could satisfy a morbid curiosity to view while yet alive this monstrosity, who could deliberately plan and execute so dastardly a crime.

The coroner's jury was quickly reassembled and Mathis was brought before it. Prosecuting Attorney Roane spoke to Mathis, admonishing him that no officer had any right to make him talk, and that nothing said by him under threat or forced from him in any way other than by a voluntary statement could legally be used against him.

Long after these events took place, Pete Ramey's daughter, Marvel Ramey Sisk, would add her own descriptions of the scene:

> At 11:20 Thursday morning Will Mathis was brought to Oxford under heavy guard. His armed escorts were Deputy Sheriff Pete Ramey, Dick Oliver, Tom Ragland, Bob Harkins, and a Mr. Sullivan. After a brief but searching examination by the coroner, the jury, and attorneys Sivley, Roane, and Stone, he was taken to jail. An immense crowd of people from all parts of the county and surrounding counties had assembled in town, and the sight of the prisoner aroused their indignation to such a pitch that it was with difficulty the calmer citizens restrained the mob from lynching the prisoner on the spot. Thursday night great crowds still thronged the streets, and ominous threats showed the general trend of sentiment.

With so many tired, angry, and armed men around the square, and a suspect in hand, the customary elements were all in place for a lynching. Many times over the course of the next year the threat of such violence would boil up, only to be quelled by calm and persuasive men who did not want Oxford to savagely erupt in the same way so many communities had. On this first morning, when the monster was in their grasp, a spark might well have lit the fuse. Rumblings and murmurs swirled around the old courthouse all through the day.

In the square, M. A. Montgomery, the United States district attorney, spoke to the crowd. He was followed by W. A. Roane, the state district attorney, who pledged a speedy, impartial, and fair trial and his best efforts to the end that justice would be done. He said that the evidence already secured would guarantee Mathis would receive his just punishment at the end of the rope with the trap sprung by the sheriff. Following this, the Reverends Porter, Bacon, and King made emotional speeches, counseling submission to the law and stating that they did not believe they were looking in the faces of murderers. The crowd took the speeches quietly and were particularly appreciative of the promise of a speedy trial.

Fortunately, at nine o'clock the one person with the power to exert the most influence rode into town. Judge Perrin H. Lowrey, presiding judge of the district, arrived, having driven thirty miles through the country from his home at Batesville. The good judge then took his turn making a speech to the people, promising that he would immediately call an extra session of the circuit court to convene in the twenty days prescribed by law for the purpose of promptly trying the Mathis case. As he talked, the people who were trying to restore order—to stopper the rumbling volcano—mingled with the crowd, pleading with them to allow the law to run its course. Mrs. Sisk reported: "By 11:00 P.M. the crowd had disappeared, and by 10:00 o'clock the next morning the town had quieted down." This action of Judge Lowrey had a signal effect on the people, and the earnest thanks of the law-abiding members of the community were expressed to him.

Nevertheless, the tension remained. The next day the *Commercial Appeal* in Memphis would report the ongoing hostilities in Oxford:

> Tonight forty men armed with shotguns and Winchesters are guarding the jail here in which are confined Will Mathis and the three accomplices implicated in the murder of the Montgomerys. The guard is under the command of Deputy Sheriff Pete Ramey, who is acting instead of Sheriff Harkins, who is sick. This preparation for a defense of the jail was preceded this afternoon by the removal of Mrs. Mathis from the jail, where she was confined. If it came to the worst the officers did not want her to witness her husband's seizure by the mob. Crying bitterly, she was led to a house where

Judge Perrin H. Lowrey

Mature Judge Lowrey

her mother is stopping. She seemed to have a premonition of the cause of her removal. She will probably be released under $1,000 bond in a few days if she can get securities. This afternoon Bill Jackson, one of the Jackson boys suspected of being accessory to the murder, was released under $1,000 bond for his appearance as a witness, but his brother was retained.

The leading citizens of the town have been making herculean efforts to stem the rising tide of lawlessness tonight and the indications are that they have been successful. Judge Lowrey made a stirring appeal from the court house steps and other citizens circulated among the excited knots of men and calmed them with the assurance of a speedy punishment. However, the embers are still smoldering and a fire may break from them at any time within the next few days.

Tonight the most violent and determined crowd was a delegation from Pontotoc, which has been helping to hunt Mathis for the last few days and which evidently hates to return without exacting vengeance for the murder of Deputy Hugh Montgomery, who was from that place.

A number of the best citizens were anxious to ship the five prisoners off on the afternoon train to Holly Springs for safekeeping, but it would seem that the crowd would not permit the removal without a struggle.

Some of the good citizens of the Delay community were outraged that their one neighborhood was repeatedly singled out by newspaper reporters as the spawning ground of all that was evil in Lafayette County. Finally, the principal of the school there could stand it no longer and sent his views to the editor of the *Oxford Eagle*:

> Delay, Miss., Dec. 22d, 1901.
> Ed. Eagle:
> In simple justice to myself as well as the citizens of Delay, I wish to be heard through the columns of the *Eagle* in regard to a communication sent the *Eagle* some time ago, in which I sought to correct a mistake as to the locality in which the Montgomerys were killed.

I had not thought of reflecting, in the least, upon the good intentions of the *Eagle*, in stating that the scene of the crime was near Delay.

But as the citizens of Delay were in no sense implicated, and as the scene of the crime was really nearer some other places than Delay, simply as a matter of information to the public I wrote giving as best I could the real facts in the case.

In its weekly issue the Eagle would take the opportunity to appeal to the public for a greater vigor in stamping out several evils that had plagued Lafayette County for so many years:

> The recent horrible murder and burning of the bodies of the murdered men in our county, should be a lesson to our citizens to make war upon vice before it becomes a menace to life and safety. For years wildcat stills and accompanying evils have existed in Lafayette county, and only spasmodic attempts have been made to rid the community of their baleful influence. The effects of this lawlessness is shown in the recent attempt to bring Mathis to punishment for various crimes. Two witnesses have been killed, others threatened and intimidated and two brave officers have given their lives attempting to enforce obedience to the law. There are more tragedies yet to come unless heroic efforts are made to clean the county of the lawless element predominating. We need united effort, determined, and unceasing effort to enforce the law, and it is the duty of every citizen to give aid in the matter.

In its November 28 issue, the *Oxford Globe* would take similar umbrage at a remark made a week earlier in the Memphis paper. The *Commercial Appeal* had called Will Mathis a bad man and went on: "He bluffed his way over the local Mississippi officials until the secret service people concluded that they had a case of counterfeiting against the man." According to the local journalist, "This assertion does our local officials an injustice, as Mathis has never turned an official down that went after him. There has never been a warrant issued in the Federal or State courts in this county that has not been promptly executed by the Sheriff or deputy marshals and the assertion made in the *Commercial-Appeal* has no foundation."

Given the public outrage, Judge Lowrey promptly acted upon his word. "A special term of the Circuit Court of LaFayette County, Mississippi, is hereby called to convene at the Court House at Oxford, in said county, on Monday, December 30, 1901, at 9 o'clock a.m., to continue for a term of twelve days, for the purpose of transacting business of a criminal nature and trying criminal cases."

By Friday morning, the 24th, everything had quieted down and the crowds had disbanded. Most people assumed that the danger of a lynching had receded. Sheriff John Harkins assured the *Commercial Appeal* correspondent that he would protect the prisoners at all hazards. Business around town, which had been at a standstill since the shocking news of the murders, resumed its normal condition. After all, Christmas was just around the corner. Students out at the university were beginning to make their vacation plans.

What was not yet known was whether the federal court would attempt to take up the cases under the charge of conspiracy to murder, since the victims had been federal agents. Anticipating a possible renewed surge of protestations from the community, US Marshal Buchanan wrote again to his superiors at the Justice Department in Washington:

> Judge Niles [Henry Clay Niles, the first judge to begin proceedings about the murders] has declined to try any of the parties mentioned, at least, for the time being, in view of the fact that a special term of our State Court has been called to meet at Oxford on December 30th, 1901, for the especial purpose of the trial of these parties. Notwithstanding the fact that they will not be tried by Judge Niles' Court, but in view of the fact that they are all indicted in the United States Court and are held as United States prisoners, I have consulted Judge Niles as directed in your said letter, who is of opinion that no attempt will likely be made to unlawfully molest said prisoners, pending the action of our State court in the premises. These prisoners are also in the custody of the Sheriff of Lafayette Co. upon the verdict of a coroner's jury. In view of the facts as stated I have concluded that the employment of a guard by the United States is unnecessary at this time.

The proclamation of a special term for the circuit court was not the only ongoing legal activity. The coroner's inquest was continued at the courthouse. Several people noted what a strictly private affair it was, and since everyone but one examined by the jury was then behind bars in the jail, the people of Oxford were left to speculate. Much would come out later of the goings-on.

Dr. W. Jones, of the University of Mississippi, had examined the body of John A. Montgomery when it was first brought to town the preceding Sunday. The doctor found undigested food just below the collarbone, which showed that the victim had been shot while eating supper or soon after. The autopsy also revealed that he had been shot in the mouth, the bullet ranging down through the stomach.

Lafayette County courthouse

At Will Mathis' trial in January, Dr. P. W. Rowland, a local physician who had participated in the examination, would give more details of the killing:

A. On the right side just under the arms the ribs were burned into.

Q. Were the ribs broken?

A. Yes, sir. The ribs on the left side were intact.

Q. On the left side were there any holes through the trunk into the cavity?

A. No, sir. I think not.

Q. Where was the hole you decided was a gunshot wound?

A. Directly over the stomach. The diaphragm was torn apart, part of it lying directly over the wound. It seemed to have been torn by a missile. . . .

Q. Did you attempt to trace the missile as it passed through the stomach?

A. Yes, sir.

Q. Did you see any wound in the liver?

A. I think not. The spleen was wounded. The membrane covering the spleen was torn. And we thought one of the kidneys was torn.

Q. What direction, judging from the different parts that were wounded, what was the general course of the missile that passed through him?

A. My idea was it was from right to left and from above downward.

Q. Could you tell without seeing the entrance and exit of a wound where it went in or where it come out?

A. No, sir.

Q. And the entrance and exit of the wound was charred?

A. Yes, sir.

Q. Did you find any shot in the body?

A. No, sir.

A few days later, at the first trial of Whit Owens, Dr. A. A. Young was called to describe the condition of John A. Montgomery's body. His version matched pretty well that of his colleague, Dr. Rowland:

Q. Tell the jury the result of your investigation.

A. We first made a general inspection and found the legs gone and the back part of the head gone and the right arm nearly in two just below the shoulder and drawn. His left arm was drawn to one side with the arm severed. The bone looked as if it had been cut with an ax or some sharp instrument.

Defense Counsel: Objected.

Objection overruled—Exception taken.

Q. Did you with others make an autopsy?

A. Yes, sir. In the body there were two holes. The body was badly charred. The openings in the body were so badly charred we could hardly tell what made the wound. We opened the chest and the abdominal cavity. There was a small opening at the top of the shoulder back of the collarbone. On opening the chest we found the lungs considerably burned, especially near the opening in the chest on the left side.

The left lung had one hole about as large as that lead pencil in it. The lower edge of the liver seemed to have had a slight abrasion and the lower end of the spleen on the left side was red as if it had been grazed by something and the upper part of the kidney looked a little red about where the diaphragm— the muscles which separate the contents of the stomach from the contents of the chest. On the left side about where the diaphragm joins the walls of the chest there was a large opening, perhaps two inches in diameter with ragged holes. . . .

Q. Tell the jury what kind of missile it was, in your judgment, that passed through.

A. Taking in connection the appearance of the hole and the wound generally it had the appearance of large shot— buckshot. . . .

Curiously, no testimony was sought concerning the body of Hugh Montgomery. His remains had been transported from the scene of his death east to his father's home, three miles south of Pontotoc. A few days after the murders of the Montgomerys, the *Pontotoc Sentinel* ran a story about Hugh Montgomery:

> On Tuesday afternoon an autopsy was ordered by District Attorney Roane to be held for identification. Coroner B. L.

Hyde, accompanied by Drs. M. R. Clark and E. N. Bigham made the examination which proved conclusively that the body was that of Hugh Montgomery. [On the witness stand the doctors would have been able to prove or disprove the statements of a witness who said Hugh Montgomery had been drinking heavily at the Mathis home.] Immediately after, it was taken to the Monroe graveyard and buried, Eld. R. A. Cooper conducting the services in the presence of a large crowd of sorrowing relatives and friends.

Hugh, the eldest son of Mr. and Mrs. William Montgomery, was born near Chesterville, this county, about twenty-six years ago. When a child his parents moved to the Porter place, a mile west of town, where they remained for some time but for a number of years they have lived on a farm in the Lochinvar neighborhood. Hugh received his education at the Pontotoc Academy and his teachers and fellow students all attest to his unusually bright, quick mind. He was a good, quiet boy, with good morals, and had developed into a worthy young man, well liked by all who knew him.

He was fearless and courageous, too brave to be intimidated by danger, when duty called him. For five years he had served as a deputy United States marshal and tho' young in years made a model officer. His shocking and untimely death is deeply regretted for his parents, only sister and two brothers.

Mr. John Montgomery was about fifty years old and leaves a wife and several children. He lived in Oxford where he had many friends who are terribly aroused at the awful death of this good citizen.

Closer to the scene of the horrible crime, the *Oxford Globe* offered more on slain officer John, publishing a poem written by an A. C. Shipp:

> John A. Montgomery.
> John A. Montgomery they say is dead, By the foul assassin's bluddy hand, That nobel Spirit from earth has fled,
> And sorrow hath filled all our land. FATHER.
> We mingle ours with the orphan's tears While in sorrow they must bow,
> Left to the world's tender cares,
> No father's hand to guide them now.

COMPANION.
Like the Spanish Oak to the vine, Sheltered from the wintry storm,
As it tenderly around it twines,
She will miss his supporting arms.
SOLDIER.
He fought for what he thought was right A tried and true southern son,
He kept his armor always bright,
His sword unsheathed and sandals on.
CITIZEN.
While in peace all else he forsook, But serve his country he must try,
His sword was beat to a prooning hook But for his country he must die.
COMRADE.
A comrade is gone from our camp, His cheery voice no more we'll hear,
No more with him on the tramp, That noble spirit that knew no fear.
FRIEND.
He is not dead nor far away, Forever near he is not gone,
He has only dropped his robe of clay, To put his shining raiment on.

Back at the coroner's inquest, Orlando Lester stated that he was sent by Mathis after a gun, and when he returned with one, Mathis tried to get Bill Jackson to help him murder the two officers. Jackson refused and tried to persuade Mathis not to do it. Lester testified that Mathis shot John A. Montgomery first and that Hugh Montgomery jumped for his pistol, which was under his pillow; as he did so, he was murdered too. Mathis then got another party, and the two bodies were dragged into a room and straw and other things piled on the bodies. All the household furniture was removed and the house set afire.

People outside the courtroom were told that more than one suspect was implicated, that authorities knew the whole plot but could not disclose any of the evidence as yet. The reporter for the *Globe* would comment on the questions flying around about the inquest: "As to the truth of the negro's disclosure we cannot vouch for it, as it is a mere rumor, but we have it from good authority and think that more than likely he has disclosed many things. It is also reported that the jury has found that the negro, who was a witness against Mathis and who was killed from ambush a few weeks ago, was killed by Luster, at the command of Mathis."

Cordie Mathis appeared before the grand jury several times, denying steadfastly that Will had anything to do with the affair and asserting over and over that her husband was innocent.

When he was safely transported to the courthouse to face the grand jury, Mathis was questioned by Roane. He said that he wanted to tell all he knew, and most of the pieces of the tale were related to the jurors. One participant in that session would long after recall that Mathis spoke in an even tone about the revolting particulars of his crime, without showing any compunction whatever. Occasionally he interspersed a sentimental remark about his wife and baby, but remorse never entered his mind except in connection with the fear of punishment. At the end he said that he only regretted three things: the burning of the two officers after the murders and his not getting a chance to kill officers Rogers and Adams.

Later he would dictate in his *Life of Will Mathis*:

> They carried me before the coroner's jury as soon as they got to Oxford with me. I made a statement before the jury, taking things on myself that Whit Owens and Arlandus Lester did themselves; I was afraid to tell the truth on them for fear the angry crowd would take them out and mob them, and while taking them take my wife, too; mobbing wasn't any too bad for them if I had thought the crowd would let my wife alone, but if a mob had gone in that jail while she was there, if some drunk had said, 'Let's take the damn woman, too,' the whole crowd would have been in for it, for a crowd of men that will go into a mob don't care for anything, just as soon do one

thing as another, so I begged for the rest in order to save my wife.

After Mathis' testified, he was taken up the street a few hundred feet to the county jail. The streets were crowded with onlookers trying to get a glance at the famous criminal. It was feared that the "jailbirds" would be hauled out and mobbed, as some people were still bent on lynching them, but the officers talked them out of any violence.

A week after Mathis was incarcerated, a reporter from the *Memphis Commercial-Appeal*, the big-city paper to the north, had a personal interview with the alleged killer:

> Through the courtesy of Sheriff Harkins, Deputy Sheriff Ramey and Jailer Ragland, a personal talk with Mathis, the principal character was secured. On entrance he was found

Lafayette County jail

lying on the bed in his cell, dictating the story of his life to a fellow convict who was taking down his remarks with as much earnestness as Boswell ever hung upon the lips of Dr. Johnson. Both agreed to submit to a slight interruption to this literary labor.

Mathis was not in quite so voluble a mood as he appeared at the coroner's inquest and told the story of his crime with such circumstantial details. However, he appears willing to answer any questions that were put to him in regard to the matter. . . .

The prisoner spoke in a low, hopeless sort of tone, as if he were thoroughly conscious that his part had been quite played out and that he had nothing to hope for.

He looked very much worried and anxious. The consciousness of his fearful condition had evidently begun to tell upon him.

"How old are you?" was asked.

"I am 26 years old. Today is my birthday," was the unexpected response.

Mathis narrated the story of his crime, laying special stress on the avowal that his wife had nothing to do with it. "She couldn't help herself, poor woman," he said, "and couldn't keep us from doing what we had made up our minds to do."

The story of his wanderings in the river bottom, with the pursuers ever at his heels and with the baying of the bloodhounds on his trail ringing in his ears, constitutes an unusually vivid chapter:

> Sunday night I slept in a cotton pen on a farm near where I lived. Next day I took to the swamp, which I knew from end to end. Monday night I slept in a cotton pen on another place, and Tuesday went back to the swamp. Tuesday they began to make a close search for me, but they never came anywhere near me. That night I slept at the home of a friend and went back to the swamp Wednesday morning.
>
> Then they began to get close in after me. I made it a point to go over the roughest ground in the swamp, because I knew that I could go faster than the ones who were following me

over that sort of ground and, further, because I knew that the dogs, if they were trained right, wouldn't go much ahead of the men for fear of getting killed. I found the plan worked to perfection. They got hot on my trail, but I had little trouble in keeping ahead of them and leading them through the roughest parts of the bottom.

Several times I had about made up my mind to stop in a good place and sell out as dearly as possible. I had a Winchester and pistol and plenty of ammunition, and was resolved not to be taken alive. Twice I thought I would have to do it whether I wanted to or not, they were so close on me. Once I was sitting on a white oak log not a hundred yards away from a crowd that was searching a crib for me. I could easily have killed several of them before they could have gotten me. They were plain marks for me and I am a good shot with the Winchester. But I kept thinking that if I got killed my wife wouldn't have any one to prove that she had nothing to do with the killing . . . .

When asked to permit the photographer to take his picture, Mathis objected that he was not suitably attired. He had on the muddy, torn clothes that he had worn during his experience in the swamp. This objection was soon overcome, and he sat docilely in the chair, with perhaps a touch of self-satisfaction, while the artist took a flashlight photograph of him. When the operation was completed he asked that two of the pictures be sent to his wife.

Orlando Lester was also photographed at this time, both pictures later appearing in the *Commercial Appeal.*

The stage was set for the most spectacular trials of the time. The crimes that had occurred in the dark of a country home would be uncovered by the light of a courtroom that would attract reporters from all over the South. The backwoods moonshiners were taking center stage.

Chapter Ten
The Judge Faces the Accused

The Federal Court of the Northern District of Mississippi convened on Monday, December 9, 1901, with Judge Henry Clay Niles presiding. His charge to the grand jury was brief and forcible, being particularly caustic about illicit retailers and distillers. He instructed the jury to investigate the recent murders of John and Hugh Montgomery, the two US marshals.

On Tuesday morning, indictments were returned against Will Mathis, Whit Owens, Orlando Lester, Bill Jackson, George Jackson, and Cordie Mathis, as principals and accessories before and after the fact. The impression around town was that these parties would not be tried now but that Judge Niles would adjourn his court until January 15 in order to allow the circuit court to try them.

While Judge Niles was considering his options, US Attorney M. A. Montgomery was preparing to try the cases. He seems to have had a great deal of volunteer assistance from local attorneys, as this request he sent to the US Attorney General indicates:

> ... [A]s three members of the bar here have given a personal interest to the prosecution as much as if they were themselves the Prosecuting Attorneys, I desire to be allowed to employ them as Assistant Counsel in the case. This will do much to allay the suspicion which is wide spread that every effort will not be made to bring the defendants to a speedy trial. The people of the county—and for that matter the people of three counties—are very much wrought up over the matter, and it will take great pressure to keep down a mob. . . .

I therefore most earnestly recommend that you allow me the amount named for the attorneys named. I do not do this because of any fear that they will not be successfully prosecuted, but that justice may be done deserving men who have given earnest assistance, and because it will teach violators of the law that the authority of the United States must be respected.

It was determined that the accused in the Montgomery murders would be tried before Judge Perrin H. Lowrey. Will Mathis finally acknowledged that he had shot at Dave Rogers two years before. That matter had remained a mystery until his confession.

C. E. Slough, clerk of the circuit court, recorded the following concerning the first day of the special term:

> The Grand Jurors of the State of Mississippi, elected, impaneled, sworn, and charged to inquire in and for the body of LaFayette County at the December Special Term, A.D. 1901, of the Circuit thereof in the name and by the authority of the State of Mississippi on their oath present that Will Mathis, Orlandus Lester, Whit Owens, and Wm. Jackson late of the County aforesaid on the 16th day of Nov. 1901, in said County unlawfully willfully feloniously and of their malice aforethought did kill and Murder John Montgomery a human being against the peace and dignity of the State of Mississippi.

The next day the four were arraigned, and each pleaded not guilty. The court thereupon ruled that they would be given "several and separate" trials. They were asked if they had counsel. Judge Z. M. Stephens and his son, of New Albany, were to represent Whit Owens. D. M. Kimbrough, a member of the faculty and then dean of the University Law School, was appointed by the court to represent Mathis. And J. W. T. Falkner, the grandfather of the novelist William Faulkner, and T. H. Somerville were appointed to defend Orlando Lester. That meant that the accused were well represented by a cadre of significant barristers.

Judge Stephens, among them, would go on to be a district attorney and a member of the state legislature. His fame as a defense attorney, which was his favorite pursuit, was legendary. For one thing, he never made notes. When working with another lawyer, Reuben Davis of Aberdeen, he had been impressed that Davis never used notes, so he adopted the same practice. Stephens asked for a change of venue for Whit Owens, but initially it was not granted, owing to the feeling of the people in regard to the accused men. In time, though, Owens would get a change of venue—twice.

The first of the accused brought to the bar was Orlando Lester. Among the instructions given by Judge Lowrey to the jury was this one:

> The Court instructs the jury for the State that any person who knowingly aids and assists in the committing of a murder is guilty of murder although he may not have struck the fatal blow or fired the fatal shot, and in this case if you believe from the evidence beyond a reasonable doubt that Orlandus Lester knowingly and willingly aided and assisted in procuring the weapons knowing the purpose for which it was to be used or knowing and willingly aided and assisted in any way in the killing of John Montgomery and that such killing was murder, although you may believe from the evidence that someone else fired the fatal shot.

The first witness was Cordie Mathis, who said that Lester had killed both the officers. She testified that he had been in her room and heard her husband, who was holding a light for the officers to get in bed, arguing with the Montgomerys. He then ran in the room and killed both the officers. This would be the first of many contradictions of earlier statements made by most of the principals. During her earlier examination by the coroner's jury, she had admitted to having a conversation with both Orlando Lester and her husband before the killings in which she had tried to dissuade them from committing the crime. At her husband's trial later in the week she would

Whit Owens in prsion in Rankin County, near Jackson

be sharply grilled by the prosecutor about all the conflicting versions that she had given different authorities.

When Lester was put on the stand, he stated that Bill Jackson and Will Mathis had killed the two officers. He told the story about going for the gun at Whit Owens' house, where Owens had given him shells and told him to be sure the officers were killed. He admitted that he had held the lamp while Mathis shot Hugh Montgomery with the Winchester and Bill Jackson shot John A. Montgomery with a shotgun.

Lester also testified that Mathis had written him a letter since they had been incarcerated. According to him, Mathis asked him in the letter if Lester would confess that he did the killing and take the blame. If so, Mathis promised, when released, to stir up a mob and free Lester before he could be hung.

All the witnesses were examined in a single morning, and the case of Lester argued in the afternoon. At 4:10 the jury retired to the jury room, and after only twenty minutes of deliberation, they returned the verdict of guilty as charged of murder in the first degree.

On February 11 the circuit clerk would record the following:

> I, C. E. Slough, the clerk of said court, do hereby certify that at a term of the said court, beginning on the 30th day of December A.D. 1901, and adjourning on the 15th day of January A. D. 1902, Orlandus Lester, the defendant, was convicted of Murder and was sentenced to be hung on the 14th day of February, A. D. 1902, and that said defendant has taken an appeal to the supreme court of the state, making oath to his inability to give cost bond or to deposit a sufficient sum of money to pay said costs. . . .
>
> [H]e [will] be taken from said jail by the Sheriff of this LaFayette County and within closure around said jail unless the Board of Supervisors shall designate some other place according to law, between the hours of 11 o'clock A.M. and 4 o'clock P.M. on said day he be hanged by the neck until he be dead.

As suggested by the date Slough recorded the above, Judge Lowrey would not immediately pass sentence on Lester until the completion of the trials of the others implicated in the matter. He did take the occasion to appoint J. E. Holmes and J. H. Kimmons to represent Bill Jackson, and that case was set for the next Monday.

One of the more intriguing aspects of the notorious dual murders is the twin nature of its leading culprit, Will Mathis. While he could be recklessly defiant, as he was on that fatal night, he also showed frequent concern for his loved ones. He had turned himself in to spare his wife, Cordie. He would not testify at the upcoming trial of Whit Owens because he was Cordie's father. He also worried about what his baby son and parents would think of him in the years to come.

Before his trial, Mathis dictated letters to *New Orleans Picayune* reporter Jennifer Standifer that he desired to leave to his parents and son. The newspaper writer was requested to leave out all provincialisms of speech and "to write it nice," and the request was complied with.

To Baxter Cleveland Mathis:

My Dear Son: It is with a heart full of sadness that I write you this from the county jail where I am now confined. I am in an iron cell 8 by 16 feet, where I am kept day and night. Everything in the room is a stove, an iron bedstead, a hard mattress and some blankets. If you live to be old enough, I want you to visit the place where your father spent his last days, and let my fate be a lesson to you. My cell is the second one on the right. As you look in, I hope that you will realize that right here I spent many an hour of fear and anguish on account of your welfare. Many a time I have hugged you to my breast, and while I loved you with all the tender affection that a father can feel for his baby, I had rather you had died in infancy than to follow the life I have led. One thing that is the earnest wish of your loving father is that you do right in all things from the time you are old enough to know right from wrong. Love and obey your kind mother and try to be a comfort to her, and make up for the trouble I have caused her. Your life will be just what you make it. You can make it a success or a failure. You will find that people will watch you closely on account of what your father has done. But you will get credit when you do right, and condemnation when you do wrong.

You will meet with evil temptations but never submit to the first temptation to do wrong. Be industrious and economical; love and fear God, and success will crown your efforts. Remember that poverty does not degrade you or make you unhappy. Nothing will degrade you but sin. The wages of sin is death. Above all never touch whiskey or any strong drink. Never think that you can take one drink without it harming you. Every drunkard has seen the time when he could let the drink alone. Intemperance has ruined more men than every other evil in the world. When whiskey gets the advantage of a man, he is fit for no business or position in life. All the demons of hell combined could not contrive or invent anything that would be a worse curse to humanity and work for Satan as whiskey. And I want to say here that women could put whiskey and drinking down if they tried.

When I was young my life was promising, I was the idol of my parents, and well thought of by everybody. There was nothing to keep me from growing up a good man, but I learned to love whiskey. At first I wanted only to take a social drink with friends, but I kept on taking it until the appetite grew on me and I could not stop. It led me to where I am now. Never touch it, my boy. Remember your father's warning, and grow up a good man. Forgive me the wrong I have done you. Your loving father,

WILL MATHIS.

The same reporter copied Mathis' letter to his parents, Samuel and Eliza, in Houlka. Years before, after Mathis had taken to running around with a rough element in Chickasaw County, they had brought him on a mule to Lafayette County and left him with relatives. Sadly, they learned that a change in geography does not guarantee a shift in character.

> To Mr. and Mrs. Samuel Mathis:
> My Dear Father and Mother: I want you to know how sorry I am that I have given you so much trouble. I know that I have broken your hearts, but the cause of my going wrong was not because you did not do your duty in bringing me up. You both did all you could to make me a good man, and after I got to drinking and got on the downward track, you both did all you could to get me to lead a better life. I don't want either of you to blame yourselves for what I have done and what you couldn't help. If you live until my boy is old enough, I want you to warn him against drinking wine or whiskey. They lead to all other sins and have brought me where I am. I have been reading my Bible and trying to make peace with God. I hope my sisters will be the comfort to you in your old age that I ought to have

been, and repay your love better than I have done. Forgive me, if you can, for bringing you so much trouble.

Your son, WILL MATHIS.

The remorse he evinced in these letters would do him no good when he was brought to the bar of justice on Thursday, January 9. He was represented by D. M. Kimbrough, assisted by Charles Hillman Brough, from Clinton, Mississippi, and J. H. Mize, from Forrest, Mississippi, both members of the university law school. While using two students as assistants may seem curious, they were both seniors. Mathis was prosecuted by District Attorney W. A. Roane, who was aided by James Stone, J. C. Wilson, C. L. Sivley, and US District Attorney M. A. Montgomery.

The first witness placed on the stand was Deputy US Marshal Frank Matthews, who testified that the Montgomerys were sent to arrest Mathis. Matthews was the office deputy, whose boss, US Marshal George M. Buchanan, was confined at his home in Holly Springs, where he had been ill for several days. Matthews took charge of the case that awful Sunday morning, and amid the frenzy he was unable to call his superior until well into the afternoon. In fact, Marshal Buchanan was never able to visit the scene of the crime, a fact that would lead some citizens to protest all the way to the president of the United States.

> **Q.** What day did they [Hugh and John Montgomery] leave Oxford for the execution of the writ?
> **A.** Saturday, the 16th of November, between 2 and 3 o'clock.
> **Q.** Do you know how far Will Mathis lived from here?
> **A.** About 12 miles in Lafayette County, Mississippi.
> **Q.** What was the charge against Mathis?
> **A.** Distilling.
> **Q.** Did you have any other business related with Hugh Montgomery passing the writ to him?
> **A.** Yes. I loaned him a Colt pistol No. 38 caliber.
> **Q.** Did you ever get that pistol back?

A. Yes, sir, several days after that I did.
Q. What was the condition of the pistol when you got it?
A. It had a good deal of blood on it.
Q. Did you ever see Hugh or John A. Montgomery after they left here that Saturday afternoon?
A. Only their remains.
Q. What did you find on arriving there?
A. The house burned down and two human bodies in it.
Q. What was the condition of the bodies?
A. They were badly burned.
Q. Who gave you that pistol back?
A. My father.
Q. Was that writ ever returned to the office or any report made as to it?
A. No, sir.

Matthews might have mentioned other federal charges that had been lodged against Mathis. According to the *Commercial Appeal*, Mathis had come under suspicion again for his counterfeiting activities. The Secret Service Division, originally created in 1865 to suppress counterfeit currency, had filed charges on November 18, while he was still on the run:

> Mathis was possessed of a reputation that would serve him well as the marshal of a boom town in the far West. . . . [T]he secret service people concluded that they had a case of counterfeiting against the man. Then the Birmingham agent of the secret service concluded to take a flyer for the counterfeiter.
>
> Mathis showed that he did not intend to be taken and the secret service man took a shot at the culprit, which succeeded in bringing him into a peaceful state of mind. He was given a preliminary hearing and bound over to the court, and H. C. Dickey, the secret service man, said yesterday [November 18] that Mathis was either now under bond for appearance at Federal Court, or had already had his hearing and been acquitted; which state of affairs existed he did not know.
>
> Mathis was a silver dollar operator, and had been accused of manufacturing dollars at various times and places. He was under surveillance by the secret service people.

Ellen Welch, Mathis' neighbor, testified to having heard the gun shots and seeing the house burning. She had seen the bright reflection of the fire on her own walls. In one of the later trials of Whit Owens, she would testify that her windows had no glass but that the light from the blaze seeped through the cracks of the closed shutters. Asked by Mr. Roane what she did the next day, she recalled the discovery of the bodies in the still burning rubble of the house.

Among the questions asked of Mrs. Welch in cross-examination by D. M. Kimbrough were those that alluded to the murder of Hampton Williams:

> **Q.** Had you prior to that heard any conversation in the neighborhood as to the killing of some negroes and who were charged with killing them?
> **A.** I heard the negroes were killed but not particular who killed them.
> **Q.** Had you heard in a general way of any suspicion against anybody?

The State immediately objected, and that line of questioning was abandoned.

Mrs. Welch would have a somewhat different story to tell at Whit Owens' trial the following week. One detail she would add is that the bodies of the two officers were carried to her house before they were sent to Oxford and Pontotoc. At that trial, no mention was made of the fact that she claimed to have heard gunfire at three separate times during the night of November 16.

> **Q.** State if you heard anything that night after supper.
> **A.** Yes, sir. Between 9 and 10 o'clock—nearer 10, I heard two large guns.
> **Q.** That night?
> **A.** Yes, sir.
> **Q.** Knock on the table and indicate how close together those shots fired.
> **A.** Knock (1-2-3-4-5-6-7-8) knock.

Q. Can you tell whether those were guns or pistols?
A. They were guns.
Q. Could you tell whether they were indoors or out of doors?
A. No, sir.
Q. Had you gone to bed?
A. Yes, sir. I had gone to bed at 10 o'clock.
Q. Did you hear anything after that?
A. Yes, sir. At 2 o'clock in the night I heard two more large guns.
Q. How do you know it was 2 o'clock?
A. I looked at the clock to see.

Other people testified to hearing shooting at two different times, claiming that the first time was when Mathis supposedly shot in the backyard when Lester returned from the Owens errand, the second time when the officers were actually shot. But only Ellen Welch would add that third, 2:00 a.m. shooting, which under the circumstances does not appear to make any sense. Perhaps, in that lawless neck of the woods, she heard another party.

Orlando Lester was called next and gave the same version of the killing that he had given in his own trial, with the exception of his statements in regard to Whit Owens. He denied that Owens gave him shells, loaded with buckshot, or that Owens sent any messages to Mathis in regard to the killing. District Attorney Roane pressed him closely about where he had gotten the gun and the shells for it. This detail would prove valuable in establishing the complicity of Whit Owens in the murders.

Later, on the stand as a witness for the State in Whit Owens' first trial, Lester again clearly contradicted himself on several occasions, leading to challenges by defense counsel as well as prosecutors. The defense wanted to swear in witnesses who could testify that they heard Lester say that Owens had not given him any shells. Incidentally, in this testimony Lester admitted that a four- or five-year-old boy at George Mask's house had seen him take the shotgun.

(The district attorney asked him at a later trial if George Mask was at home at the time, and Lester said he was not. Then Roane asked if any of the family were there, and Lester said that they were in the kitchen eating supper. The judge would not allow the defense to put those witnesses on the stand.)

Through most of the trials, Lester would maintain that Owens either had nothing to do with the killing of the marshals or that he only provided the shells and told Lester where to get the shotgun. Finally, however, at the first retrial for Owens in Holly Springs, the defense counsel would make great effort to show Owens' benign intentions:

> **Q.** You said awhile [sic] ago that you had been living with Whit Owens for three or four years. I want to ask you if you know Henry Thompson, a yellow negro who lived in that country?
> **A.** Yes, sir. I knew him.
> **Q.** Didn't the defendant here [Owens] say to you in his presence, in the presence of Henry Thompson, a short time before this trouble that you had to keep away from Will Mathis and quit drinking whiskey and living around Will Mathis, and didn't he threaten to whip you if you didn't keep out of such company?

Further attacking Lester's credibility, Roane spent some time exposing the contradictions among the various tales that Lester had told since being captured, trying to trap the man in his own web.

> **Q.** Do you know that this is not your case being tried?
> **A.** Yes, sir.
> **Q.** Do you know that anything said here cannot be used against you any further?
> **A.** Yes, sir.
> **Q.** Is what you are telling the truth?
> **A.** Yes, sir.
> **Q.** Have you told it all just as it occurred?
> **A.** Yes, sir.

Q. Haven't you changed it any?
A. I suppose not.
Q. Have you made the same statement all the time?
A. I think I have.
Q. You didn't make any different statement to Mrs. Standifer in the jail?
A. Yes, sir. I suppose I did.
Q. Don't you know you did?
A. Yes, sir.
Q. What did you tell her?
A. She asked me if I done that shooting and I told her I did.
Q. What made you tell her that? Was that the truth?
A. No, sir.
Q. What made you tell a story then?
A. Mr. Mathis told me to tell her.
Q. You will do anything he tells you to do, will you?
A. No, sir. I wouldn't do anything he told me to do.
Q. Were you afraid of him?
A. No, sir.
Q. You just did it for accommodation then?
A. He told me if I did that that would clear him and he would get out and would take me out.
Q. You believed that, did you?
A. I didn't know.
Q. You thought you would run the risk?
No answer.
Q. Who are you trying to clear now? You can't clear yourself.
A. I ain't trying to clear anyone.
Q. You are not working under anybody else's influence now?
A. No, sir.
Q. Nobody has got you to tell this tale you are telling this evening?
No answer.
Q. How about that?
A. No, sir. I guess not.
Q. Are you sure of it?
A. Yes, sir.
Q. Didn't you say yesterday in your own trial that Mr. Owens gave you some shells?
A. Yes, sir. I said that.
Q. Why did you say that then?
A. I don't know.

Q. Just for fun?

A. I don't know.

Q. Did you have anything different to make you tell the truth yesterday from what you have today?

A. No, sir. I guess not.

Q. Didn't you make a drawing showing the position of the house and the men in the bed and with yourself with the gun holding it?

A. Yes, sir.

Q. At whose instance did you make that?

A. Mr. Mathis.

Q. Didn't you know when you drew that and made that statement and admitted the killing that it would affect your case?

A. No, sir.

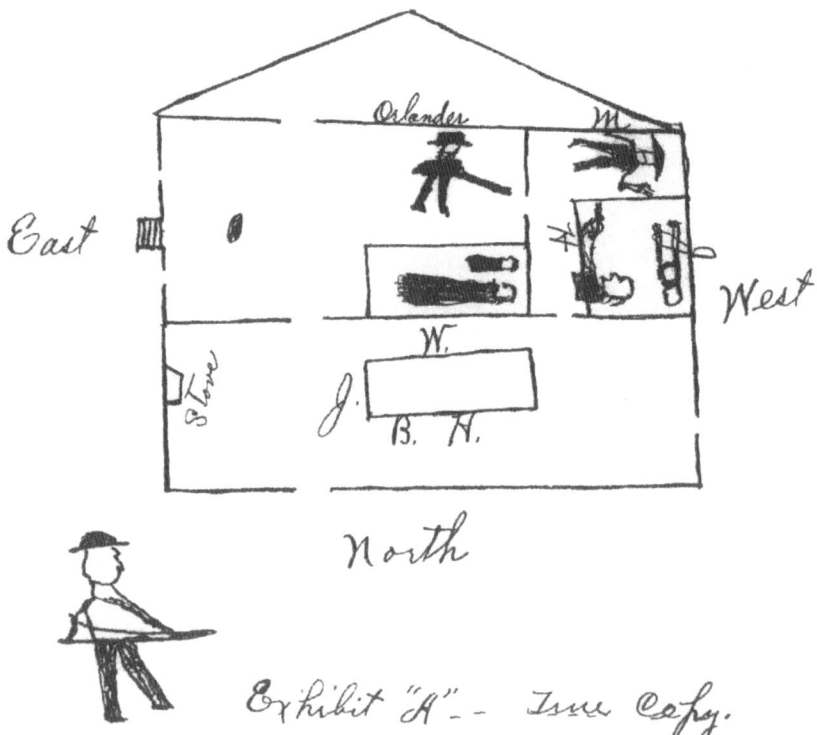

Sketch of the murder scene drawn by Orlando Lester

Q. You have no motive then for anything you say?
A. I don't understand.
Q. Have you any reason for saying what you do beside telling the truth this evening? Has anybody told you they would get you out if you would tell this tale?
A. No, sir.
Q. Or keep you from being hung?
A. No, sir.
Q. How many different statements have you made about this thing?
A. I don't know, sir.
Q. You have admitted making three, haven't you?
A. I don't know as I have.
Q. You admitted that you told Mrs. Standifer a different tale and you admitted that you told a different tale yesterday in your trial and the one you told this evening makes three?
A. Yes, sir.
Q. What made you go after that gun?
A. Mr. Mathis told me to go after it.
Q. Was that the only reason?
A. Yes, sir.
Q. Where did he tell you to go?
A. He told me to go to Mr. Owens' and to George Mask's.
Q. What did Mr. Owens tell you when you got to his house?
A. He didn't tell me anything. Only told me to go ahead and wait until I come back and he would tell me more about it.
Q. More about what?
A. More about going back up there.
Q. When you come back what did he tell you?
A. He told me to tell Mr. Mathis he couldn't come. He said his folks would alarm the country.
Q. Did he give you anything to take back to Mr. Mathis?
A. No, sir.
Q. You are sure of that?
A. Yes, sir.
Q. Positive, are you?
A. Yes, sir.
Q. You were just as positive yesterday that he did give you something to take back with you.
A. No, sir. He didn't give me nothing.

Further along in the trial, even the defense lawyer could not get him to admit to having told different stories at different times. While Orlando Lester could not be described as the most honest person, since a man might be known by the company he keeps, he had no reason to tell conflicting versions of that night's events. He had already been convicted. He had nothing more to lose. So why would he want to protect Whit Owens? Why would he want to condemn Bill Jackson? The answers to these questions would remain one of the mysteries of this case.

Chapter Eleven
The Damning Testimony

The prosecution was hardly finished with making its case against Will Mathis. One after another came the parade of damning witness statements. One of the most severe blows would be delivered by a friend that Mathis hoped would help cover his tracks.

Shell Vines, who had seen Mathis the day after the murder at his brother Ken's house, took the stand next for the State. At the time Mathis spoke to him on the night of the murders, Vines did not know about the killings or the burning of the house.

Mathis asked Vines to swear that Will had stayed at Ken Vine's place, and that Shell Vines saw him there on Saturday night. When asked why, Mathis said the revenuers had come out to his house and that he gave them a "high ball" and got away. At one of the Owens trials, the district attorney would press Shell Vines closely as to what a "high ball" was, asking if it were a drink of some sort. Not used to drinking anything but moonshine, Vines answered, "I understood the high ball he gave was the dodge he gave them. I never taken a drink called a high ball."

Vines said he told Mathis, "They will take you up," since he was already under bond for his appearance at court. Mathis replied that he didn't want to go to jail till his trial came up and he would avoid the officers. Vines remained reluctant to commit perjury, however, saying he couldn't swear to anything, because he didn't know where Mathis had stayed the night before.

"I told him I never saw you till just awhile [sic] ago and

then he said that wasn't all of it. And I asked him again what he had done that he wanted me to make such testimony and he didn't say. He said his house might have burnt up the night before and that the damn sons of bitches were in it."

On cross-examination, D. M. Kimbrough asked for more details about the conversation. "Is there anything you have failed to tell that Mathis said to you?"

Mathis had related to Shell Vines, as he did to others, that he was cleaning a hog. Then Vines added a new detail: "He said he asked Jackson to help his wife dress the hog, that he was going to step off and then he said his wife come to where he was and he told her to go get his pistol and bring it to him, that he was going to get away. And he said she went back and opened the bureau drawer and wrapped it up in the baby's clothes and brought it to him. And then he told her to go get ready and he would carry her to her father's, and she come back and he carried her."

> **Q.** Did he say whether or not the officers were killed?
> **A.** No, sir. He said it might have been.
> **Q.** He didn't say where he killed them?
> **A.** No, sir.
> **Q.** Did Mathis say anything to you about the negro's difficulty or being afraid of the officers that were after him?
> **A.** No, sir. Not that I recollect. I wouldn't firmly say he didn't.
> **Q.** Are you related in any way to the Jacksons?
> **A.** I reckon not. My brother married Bill Jackson's daughter.

George Jackson was called next. His version was in line with Mathis' first statement in regard to the killing, in which Mathis said that he did the shooting himself. He had planned to have Orlando Lester do the shooting, but Lester's nerve failed him. According to Jackson, Mathis had killed Hugh Montgomery first, shooting him in the mouth; he ended up having to shoot John A. Montgomery twice, once in the body and once in the head.

After some questions and answers about the details of the

killings, District Attorney Roane began to ask Jackson about the pistols and other items Mathis had allegedly taken from the dead officers.

> **Q.** Did you say he buried the pistols?
> **A.** No, sir. I hid them under a clay root.
> **Q.** Did the men force you to tell where they were?
> **A.** They asked me and I told. There was a crowd of them and they was talking every which way and I told them.
> **Q.** Without any further provocation?
> **A.** Yes, sir.
> **Q.** Didn't they tell you what they would do to you if you didn't tell them?
> **A.** They was talking pretty rough and I told them. They never even asked me about the knife and cartridges but I told them.
> **Q.** Why did you hide the pistols?
> **A.** I hid them because I knowed they would be called for and I wanted them where nobody else could get them and I had no chance to put them in a safer place at that time.

The district attorney went on to probe about his brother, Bill Jackson. When he asked if George had ever been convicted of any crime, such as illicit distilling, he firmly denied it. "We never had any trouble in our lives."

> **Q.** You haven't any prejudices against him for testifying against your brother?
> **A.** No, sir. Mr. Mathis is a man I never had any dealings with much. He was always good and kind to me. We pass and repass and never had any trouble in our lives.

The next witness to be called to the stand was Dr. P. W. Rowland. The prosecution wanted him to testify about the condition of the corpse of John A. Montgomery. His grisly description was certain to enrage any decent citizen, confirming that John Montgomery had been violently shot and his body burned.

As with so many aspects of the Montgomery killings, various witnesses offered more or less information from trial to trial, often with no challenge from prosecuting or defense attorney. At one of Owens' trials, Dr. A. A. Young had this exchange with the district attorney concerning the autopsy on John Montgomery:

Q. Where did you make this examination at?
A. I think in what is known as the witness room of the courthouse, the southwest corner room of the second story.
Q. And that was about how far from where the killing occurred?
A. I think about 11 miles. I may be mistaken.
Q. About how long after the killing did you make this examination?
A. It was within two or three days. I don't remember just what day. Monday or Tuesday.
Q. Did anyone assist you in the examination?
A. Yes, sir.
Q. Did you examine the back of this man? You refer to the front parts of the body. Did you examine the back?
A. No, sir. It was not turned over.
Q. You couldn't say whether or not he was shot in the back or whether the shot entered in the back or not?
A. Not from personal knowledge.

It is a sign of the primitive nature of forensics at the time that the doctors did not roll the body over and check for wounds, exit or entry. Such an examination might have greatly helped establish the victim's position at the time of the shooting.

The final witness the State called was Jennifer Standifer. When asked by Roane in what capacity she was acting when she spoke with Mathis, she replied, "I was acting as correspondent for the *New Orleans Picayune*. They telegraphed me to get a sketch of his life from him if possible and I did so." Roane asked her for other information that Mathis had shared with her.

Q. Tell the jury what he said about his connection with the killing.

A. He volunteered the statement that he didn't do the killing. He said that Orlandus Lester did it. He said he could have prevented it if he had wanted to but that he did not do the shooting. He repeated that several times.

Q. What part did he say he did?

A. I didn't ask him. I asked him where he was born and who his father and mother were and about his career in life.

Q. Did you ask him whether or not he was armed?

A. I asked him if he was drunk on the evening of the killing. He said he was pretty full of whiskey, that he had been drinking all the afternoon but that he wasn't so full that he didn't know what he was doing and that he treated them right and got them to stay.

Q. Did he say he was present when the killing occurred?

A. No, sir.

Q. Was there anything said by him about the light, as to who held the light?

A. I think he said he held the lamp but I am not certain. But I am certain that he said he did not do the shooting. He said Hugh Montgomery had mistreated him and threatened his life and that others had threatened his life and that he carried a pistol and was obliged to carry it and that Hugh Montgomery had taken this pistol away from him and that he had paid $20 for it and that that was what the fuss was about.

Finally, it was the turn of the Defense to call witnesses: Will Mathis took the stand. He denied all his previous statements, claiming they were made under promise of assistance or threats of bodily harm. During cross-examination, he would not have such an easy time. The district attorney asked incredulously, "When you were surrounded by the officers of the law and when you were in the county Courthouse, you then told the tale that you participated in the killing. Was that when you were scared?"

Mathis answered, "Yes, sir. I was scared all the time."

In discussing the disposition of the items taken from the Montgomerys, Mathis similarly cited fear as the driving force behind what he now claimed was an untrue statement he made in front of the coroner's jury. When questioned about it, why had he claimed to have taken Hugh Montgomery's watch and given it to Whit Owens to pass along to his son? "I tried to think of what was the best thing to tell to save my life," Mathis contended.

After much back and forth as to what he had told the coroner's jury that contradicted what he was telling the present jury, counsel for the defense objected and said that Roane could not ask questions related to that event because Mathis had not been under oath.

Undeterred, near the end of Mathis' testimony, the district attorney introduced a letter that Mathis had allegedly written:

> Mr. Shell Vines:
> I will write you this statement. I want you to tell that I came to Ken's Sunday morning, and that I told you and Ken that Orlandus Lester had killed Hugh and John Montgomery and burned them and that I never had anything to do with it, that I was holding the lamp for them to go to bed, and I got into a fuss with Hugh about my pistol and the negro jumped in the door and shot them and that I told you all that the negro slipped around my house trying to kill them unbeknowing to me, but he failed. I went in the yard and the negro made a signal to me but I thought he said 'Shoot' and i thought it was somebody trying to get to kill me and I shot at him and he then let himself be known and told his name. I told him he should not do it for they were just doing their duty as officers and made him go after some wood for me. I told you all that I would go and tell it but they had some papers for me and I was afraid they would put me in jail. And I thought I would dodge until court so if they put me in jail I wouldn't have to stay long. Tell that I never made any secret of it at all. That I said I would tell it if I was called. Tell that I showed you some pistols and you asked me what I was going to do with them. I told you all that I aim to give John Montgomery's pistol to his people and I aimed to keep the other two. I am going to have you and Ken summonsed to swear this for me. This was the first statement that I made and if you all swear it they will have to

take it. I am going to swear that Orlando slipped off and got a gun and came back and tried to kill the men unbeknowing to me but failed. That some of us kept in his way and that I went out after some wood and he said 'Shoo' for me to come to him and I thought he said 'Shoot' and I shot at him, thinking it was somebody aiming to kill me. He let hisself be known and told his name. I told him he should not do it and made him go after some wood and chop it up and I went in the house and in a few minutes the men went in to lay down and I carried the lamp in for them to see to go to bed and after they pulled their clothes off I saw my pistol and I told Hugh Montgomery he had told me a damn'd lie about my pistol and that I was going to have it and he said to me, 'God damn you. We will take you to Oxford tonight.' The negro heard this and ran in and shot them both before I knew he was in the house and we all left then and went to your Pa's and me and your Pa and the negro went back up there. There is not any use for me to tell you anything else that I am going to swear for you was not there.

If you can swear the same that I have right and not get yourself in trouble I can come clear, but I don't want you to tell anything to hurt yourself to save me. Don't let anybody know that I am going to try to beat it and that Lester is going to take it all on himself. If you all will do that I will come clear. The negro will tell he did it all and Cordie will tell the same and they won't have any witness against me. I am working the thing a damn'd sight finer than they think for. My lawyer says that this will clear me.

I have never been sworn yet. Don't let anybody know anything about this. I want to surprise them.
Your friend,
Will Mathis, Oxford, Miss.

If District Attorney Roane thought that battering the defendant would cause him to crack, he had not reckoned on the hardened criminal that Mathis had become. Time and time again, he and Roane had sharp exchanges. The transcripts from the trial show Roane's frequent moments of skepticism and just as often Mathis' blanket denials that he had anything to do with the killings. The back-and-forth fencing reached a height as the prosecutor pressed the accused as to why he needed testimony from Ken and Shell Vines.

Q. You had Shell Vines summonsed?
A. Yes, sir.
Q. What for?
A. To prove by him that I told him about them men, about them being killed here today. I told him I wanted him to swear that I stayed there that night.
Q. That was a lie, wasn't it? If they had sworn that, it would have been false?
A. Yes, sir.
Q. Yet you wanted them to do it?
A. Yes, sir. I wanted to prove myself away from home and they told me they wouldn't swear no lies for me.
Q. You wanted to prove yourself away from a place where somebody else was committing a crime even if you didn't have anything to do with it?
A. Yes, sir.
Q. You were willing to have your house and things burnt up to hide a crime that somebody else committed?
A. Yes, sir. My father-in-law was into it and I couldn't save him.
Q. How was he into it?
A. The negro stated that he sent him there and that he give him the shells and told me to kill them and he wanted me to do it. And I told him he should not do it, that they were just doing their duty as officers.
Q. He said Mr. Owens wanted him to kill them and sent you word to not let them get away?
A. Yes, sir.
Q. He sent some buck shot shells, didn't he, by Lester?
A. Yes, sir. And I told him it didn't matter a damn what Mr. Owens said. I knowed my business better than he did.
Q. You selected Shell Vines and Ken because you believed their testimony would be taken for you?
A. I knew they had got me in a bad thing and I wanted to get out the best way I could.
Q. Shell Vines didn't get you into it, did he?
A. No. And he wouldn't help me out either.
Q. Ain't you doing the same thing now: trying to get out?

A. I want to get out but I ain't doing it by telling lies.
Q. You have told several tales about it?
A. Not since I have been on the stand this time. This is the first time I have been sworn.

The district attorney then moved on to a second letter. Mathis had not disclaimed writing the first, but the exchange between the two of them about the second letter would get an angry rise out of the defendant. A handwriting expert is not required to draw the conclusion that Will Mathis almost certainly did not write it. As it was quite damning to Mathis, however, the identity of the writer bears some attention. Perhaps the term "instigator" might be more appropriate than writer. As it would emerge later, at least one person besides the Montgomery families and the State of Mississippi would have welcomed the hasty execution of Will Mathis. That was none other than his own father-in-law, Whit Owens.

Q. You say you didn't write this?
A. No, sir.
Q. It sounds mighty like you, don't it?
A. I didn't write it.
Q. Isn't that your signature?
A. That is my name, but I didn't write it.
Q. Do you think now that you are a damn sight smarter than they thought you were?
A. No, sir.
Q. Mr. Bennett was in jail with you, wasn't he?
A. Yes, sir. But he stayed with Jackson and Owens. He didn't come in and stay with me. They haven't none of them taken up with me in there. They have been in with the other crowd. He stayed with me half a day.
Q. You know Bennett?
A. Yes, sir.
Q. Ain't he the same Bennett you gave a letter to smuggle out to your wife?
A. I don't believe Bennett will testify that I ever gave him a letter.
Q. What do you say about it?

A. I say I didn't do it.

Q. Didn't you write to your wife that one Parks, a Federal prisoner, had told you that you could get saws in Memphis for twenty cents apiece and that you could get a dozen for $2.00 and that it would take a dozen to saw out of the jail and that Parks had agreed to go to Memphis to get the saws for you to saw out of jail?

A. No, sir.

Roane might not have expected such a stout denial, because he then proceeded to read aloud from the letter. From his constant asides, he clearly meant to goad Mathis into admitting that in fact he had written the letter:

Q. "Dear Cordie: It is with a sad heart and a tear in my eye I write these few lines. It is you and Clelan—" That is your baby's name?

A. Baxter Clelan.

Q. "It is you and Clelan that is troubling me. I think how happy we have been together and how sweet Clelan was to me and how I have to be taken from you and I don't know what will become of you and him. If I could just get out, I think maybe we would live together again. I don't know Aunt Bet—" You have an Aunt Bet?

A. Bill Jackson's wife's mother is aunt to my wife.

Q. You call her Aunt Bet?

[When Mathis affirmed that this was true, Roane went on:]

Q. "I don't think Aunt Bet and others can get you afraid to live with me. I wish I could see them. I would make them remember the last time they saw me and it would be the last time they would want to see me. I think people think I was mean to you and that you didn't care anything for me." How do you spell care?

A. I don't know. Do you want me to spell it? I would spell it "ker." Would you spell it "ker" or "cer"?

Q. "Cordie—there is a man in jail by the name of Parks. He is from the Mississippi bottom. He says if I will get some one [sic] to go with him to Memphis he will get some saws that I can get out of here with. I can get out with saws if they are steel hack saws, ten or twelve inches long made for sawing iron. I never told him that I could get anyone to go with him. I told him I didn't know who would go. He says he is going to get them and bring them to me if I can get someone to go with him and bring them back. They cost twenty cents apiece."

The prosecutor paused, then asked the question: "Was Parks from the Mississippi bottom?"

Mathis stubbornly denied knowing the man. "They say he was."

Not getting the answer he wanted, Roane decided to switch tracks:

> **Q.** How do you spell cents?
> **A.** SENTS I would spell it.
> **Q.** "He says it will take twelve of them to saw out. By taking twelve he says he can get them for $2.00. I have got two of my pictures for you and Clelan and if you don't get some one to get the saws, if you can't get some one [sic] to buy the saws, get George to buy a—"

Roane paused and then asked:

> **Q.** You had some pictures taken?
> **A.** A fellow come there and taken them while I was in jail.
> **Q.** He agreed to give you two?
> **A.** Yes, sir.

At this point the counsel for the defense objected to the introduction of the letters as incompetent and to all questions as to the letters, but the judge allowed Roane to proceed with his questioning.

> **Q.** You have a brother-in-law, George Mask?
> **A.** Yes, sir. But me and him don't get along.
> **Q.** "If you don't get some one [sic] to get the saws, get George to buy four half inch drills and two files and a brace and an inch auger and cold chisel and hammer. I can get out of here if I can get them. And send my pistol with them, and you come,

for it will take a good while to get out that way but I can get out. Your best love,"

The prosecutor paused once again, hoping to pierce Mathis' armor, but the defendant was more incensed than ever by this attempt to link him with an attempted break-out from jail.

Q. You wrote that, didn't you?
A. No, sir. I want to know where you got that.
Q. "I think if you will see Jim Kimball and tell him about the saws and the name of the saws and tell him to write to Newt to send the saws to him and he can fetch them to me. If I could have told Walker, I think he would have went and got them for me.
"Cordie, send my pistol to me anyhow if you can't send anything alse and send me a pint of whiskey with the pistol. If I have to fight my way out, I want to be half drunk and nothing wouldn't excite me." Will, you said all that, didn't you?
A. No, sir.
Q. It sounds mighty like you, don't it?
A. I don't know that it does.
Q. You don't get excited when you are half drunk, do you?
A. I don't get excited no time, unless it is something like they had me that day.
Q. "Be sure and get .44 cartridges." What size is the pistol your wife has of yours?
A. I ain't got none.
Q. What size is the one you had?
A. Forty one.
Q. "Be sure and get .44 cartridges for pistol and .32 Winchester cartridges for Ragland's pistol." He is the jailer? Your purpose was to kill him and get his pistol, wasn't it?
A. He didn't bring his pistol in the jail.
Q. You have been watching him then to see whether you could knock him in the head and get away.

Mathis disclaimed all knowledge of any letter written to his wife while in jail telling her to aid him to escape. He said it was all a plot of Bill Jackson's, perhaps unwilling to consider that his father-in-law might be so low. Mathis and Roane would then debate the question of his signature on the letter at some length.

>**Q.** Have you any objections to writing a little for us at our dictation?
>**A.** I don't have to write to make you believe what I said. You prove that I wrote that.
>**Q.** I want to prove it by you.
>**A.** You can't do that for I didn't write it.
>**Q.** Do you object to writing some for us?
>**A.** I ain't going to write. If you can't take my word, of course if I want to. I could turn here and write a running hand and change my hand anyway.

Under redirect examination, the argument about the authorship of the letters would continue. In this era, of course, no handwriting expert was to be found anywhere near a sleepy university town.

>**A.** I want to tell the jury that there are more men in jail beside me charged with this same thing and they have been in the cells together and they found out I was going to tell the straight thing about it and they have gone together. The other day I told Vick Richmond to tell my wife to come down to the jail, and Mr. Owens told George not to tell her to come down there, that he didn't think she ought to see me and they are all against me.
>**Q.** Have you any reason to suspect that anyone else wrote those letters to get you in trouble?
>**A.** I never thought about such a thing until now, but I believe Jackson and Bennett is the ones that done it.
>**Q.** You say you didn't give Bennett a letter to bring out to your wife?
>**A.** No, sir. And Bennett won't testify to such a thing either. I will bet my life on it. Defendant asks that he be permitted to write at the dictation of Counsel for the State if they now desire.
>**Court:** I will allow that.
>**A.** What must I write?

Roane now took over the questioning:

> **Q.** Shell Vines. [Witness writes.] I will write you this statement. I want you to tell that I come to Ken's on Sunday and that I told you and Ken that Orlandus Lester—
> **A.** I have wrote enough for you now to compare the hand writing.
> **Q.** Well, sign your name.
> **A.** W. M. Mathis.
> **Q.** Write Will Mathis. [Writes.]

Mathis' lawyer then renewed his objection to the introduction of letters as evidence in court. "The letters are not in evidence," the judge declared. "Nothing but the testimony of the witness is competent. The letters are not offered in evidence."

That this letter was not admitted into evidence would become a key factor in the ultimate settlement of Whit Owens' case, once the Supreme Court of Mississippi made its final decision.

Cordie Mathis was next called to testify for the Defense, and she repeated in substance what she had stated at Lester's trial. She denied the testimony she had given at the coroner's inquest, saying she was then laboring under great stress and did not remember what confession she had made.

In cross-examination, Roane asked her to identify her husband's writing from the samples at hand. Then he asked her about the letter that had angered Mathis and the letter to Shell Vines.

> **Q.** Did you get a letter from Will Mathis enclosing a letter in the same envelope to Shell Vines since he has been in jail, and didn't he write in that what you all were to swear?
> **A.** No, sir.
> **Q.** Did he write you a letter to get him some saws and a hammer and other tools?
> **A.** No sir. I never heard of it until this court.

Q. What is your baby's name?
A. Clelan.
Q. What is Bill Jackson's wife's name?
A. Beulah.
Q. Haven't you an Aunt Bet?
A. Yes, sir. Several. And cousins too.

Roane would continue to push Cordie on why she had given so many contradictory statements about the murders. Her main response was that she was scared. Like her husband, she wasn't giving the prosecution one blessed thing it could use. The hostile sides had one last exchange on this topic.

Q. At that time nobody had ever talked about hanging anybody, had they?
A. Yes, sir. Everybody talked about it.
Q. About hanging you?
A. Yes, sir.
Q. When you first made your statement?
A. Yes, sir. I heard it before I came to Oxford.
Q. Tell us one or two that talked about hanging you?
A. They talked of it when they put me in jail.
Q. Weren't you kept out of jail in the witness room until after you made your second statement?
A. No, sir. They put me in jail right then as soon as they brought me here.
Q. Didn't you sit down stairs in the Chancery Clerk's office until after you had been brought before the coroner's jury twice?
A. They didn't bring me but once, did they?
Q. I am not on the stand.
A. It don't seem to me like they did. They brought me on the stand and carried me back in the room and then carried me to jail.
Q. Didn't you come before the coroner's jury and deny any knowledge of the killing and deny everything about it until your father come on the stand and didn't he tell you to tell the truth after he come on the stand?
A. I don't remember.

Q. Didn't you come to town with your father?
A. Yes, sir.
Q. There were no officers with you then?
A. No, sir.
Q. You were kept here only as a witness and had been before the coroner's jury twice before you were arrested?
A. I don't think I was before them but once.

Jailer Tom Ragland was next called and identified the letters written by Mathis to his wife and friends while in jail. There followed more discussion of letters, including one that Mathis had evidently asked Ragland to deliver to a Presbyterian minister out west at College Hill. Rev. Mills was then called to the stand.

Q. You are a minister of the Gospel?
A. Yes, sir.
Q. Did you visit Mr. Mathis in jail?
A. Yes, sir.
Q. Look at that note and see whether or not you ever saw it before.
A. Yes, sir. I got this note from Mr. Ragland, the jailer, yesterday morning.
Q. Compare that letter with that note—
Court: Are you introducing him as an expert on handwriting?
Counsel for the State: Yes, sir.
Q. Are you acquainted with the handwriting of Mr. Mathis?
A. No, sir. This is the first time I have ever seen it.
[Far-fetched as it may seem, Mills ostensibly had not opened the letter from Mathis on the previous day.]
Q. Are you an expert on hand writing?
A. No, sir. Of course, I am brought in contact with a great many kinds of writing but as to being an expert, that is different.

On cross-examination, the attorney for the defense tried to point out one other problem in calling forth a preacher for a witness:

Q. You visited Mr. Mathis several times and talked with him?
A. Yes, sir.
Q. He talked with you as a confidential advisor?
A. Yes, sir.
Q. And as a preacher?
A. Yes, sir.
Q. He submitted to you what he professed to be a confession, didn't he?

Having established Mills' relationship to Mathis while the latter was imprisoned, the defense once again objected to the letters going before the jury, since Mathis wrote them in confidence to a religious counselor. But the court ruled that the letters were competent testimony.

Just before the noon recess Judge Lowrey surprised the crowd by having the jury taken out and instructing the sheriff to have every man who entered the courtroom searched in order to make sure that no weapons had been brought in. This unusual interruption was caused by a persistent rumor that the prisoners would be lynched that night. Until two o'clock Thursday morning everyone expected a lynching, but wiser counsel again prevailed and the case proceeded as scheduled.

On the last day of the trial the largest crowd of any day of the term crowded the gallery. One paper observed that the place was packed to suffocation.

After all testimony was given, US District Attorney M. A. Montgomery opened the argument for the prosecution. He was followed by Messrs. Kimbrough, Mize, and Brough, for the defense. The argument for the prosecution was closed by District Attorney Roane and the case given to the jury at 3:30 Friday afternoon. According to the lead reporter for the *Oxford Eagle*, "The speech of District Attorney Roane on this occasion was one of the most eloquent ever delivered in the court room."

It was persuasive, for after only a half hour the jury brought in a verdict of guilty as charged in the indictment.

Throughout the whole of the trial, Will Mathis had maintained a bold and defiant air, indignantly asserting his innocence. But when the closing arguments in the case began, his nerve seemed to fail him, and by the close of the case he was dejected and downcast. Each point brought out seemed to have the effect of a physical blow, and his bearing changed completely. After the jury had retired, he nervously watched the door. When the jury brought in the verdict of guilty, he broke down entirely, his bravado vanished, and he had nothing to say. His wife was deeply affected and wept bitterly.

All of his attempts to pin the murders on Orlando Lester had failed, just as Lester's strategy of blaming Will Mathis had. The two moonshiners, who separately had strong reasons to fear being arrested, had been judged by ordinary citizens and condemned regardless of who actually pulled the trigger. In the end, both of them would pay the ultimate price for the heinous crimes against officers of the law. Yet a third conspirator, the one who had told Lester to shoot the Montgomerys—at least in some of Mathis' accounts—still had to be tried.

Whit Owens was never placed at the scene of the murders. The wily older moonshiner would not be condemned in an open-and-shut trial; his lawyers would be able to drag the proceedings out over several trials. The possible mastermind of the twin murders would prove a much harder villain to bring low.

Chapter Twelve
Whit Owens Faces the Court

The court experienced great difficulty getting a jury for the first trial of Whit Owens, for the murder of John A. Montgomery. The special venire, or jury pool, was exhausted, as well as the regular panel. Seventy-three jurors were examined before twelve men acceptable to both prosecution and defense could be found competent to serve. The jury was finally secured by noon on Monday, January 13, and the trial began the next day.

Once the State had proved the physical facts in the case, Orlando Lester was put on the stand. He testified that after the Montgomerys had eaten supper, Will Mathis sent him to George Mask's house for a gun. He'd been told to come back by Whit Owens' and tell Owens to come to Mathis' and bring his gun. Lester said he did this: he retrieved the gun from the rack at Mask's, went to Owens's home, and delivered the message.

> **Q.** Did you see any of the balance of the Owens family when you were there?
> **A.** Yes, sir. I seen his wife.
> **Q.** What was she doing?
> **A.** Crying.
> **Q.** Anything else?
> **A.** No, sir.
> **Q.** Did Mrs. Owens hear anything said to you by Owens?
> **A.** No, sir. I don't reckon she did.

Evidently, Mrs. Owens heard more than Lester thought, because she threatened to tell the entire neighborhood if

Owens went to his son-in-law's house. Instead, according to Lester, Owens ordered him to tell Mathis to kill the men rather than let them get away. Lester said Owens looked at the gun, examined the shells, and said they were buckshot, the right ammunition for the job.

Lester then repeated what he had testified at earlier trials. He returned to Mathis' house, and after the officers had been put to bed in a shed room, Mathis came out in the yard and had a conference with Bill Jackson, who had come over for some whiskey. Mathis filled two bottles of liquor for Jackson and sent Lester into the room where the Montgomerys slept to get some corn cobs for stoppers. Lester said he got the cobs and was turning to leave the room when Mathis and Bill Jackson barged inside, one with a shotgun and the other with a Winchester rifle. Mathis said, "Hands up!" And when the officers began stirring in bed, both fired, killing the two Montgomerys.

Mathis, his wife, and Lester then went to Whit Owens' house and revealed what they had done. In Lester's version of subsequent events, Owens returned with Mathis and Lester to the house and checked the officers to see if they were dead. They brought a spade from Owens' house to bury the bodies, but Mathis said he would fix them. He dragged the bodies in another room, robbed them, piled the bedding on them, and set them on fire.

On cross-examination, Owens' defense attorney got Lester to admit that he had told several falsehoods about this matter.

Not so easily dispensed with was the testimony of ex-Sheriff P. E. Matthews. On the stand he testified that after a revenue officer had been shot at near Owens' house in an earlier incident, Owens declared that revenue officers had better quit bothering them, because the next ones who came out there would be killed. The testimony concerning this overheard comment would become a crucial part of Owens' appeals and the disposition of them by the Mississippi State Supreme Court.

The prosecutor proceeded to another damning detail that showed the sort of man they were dealing with. He wanted to establish that Whit Owens would stoop to stealing from the law officers after they had been killed. Jailer Tom Ragland testified that Owens confessed to hiding Hugh Montgomery's watch under Owens' barn; Ragland and other officers had gone to the place Owens had named and found the watch.

> **Q.** What official position do you hold in this county?
> **A.** Jailer and Deputy Sheriff.
> **Q.** Do you know Whit Owens, the defendant in this case?
> **A.** Yes, sir.
> **Q.** Did you have a conversation with him since he has been incarcerated in the county jail with reference to a watch said to have belonged to Hugh Montgomery?
> **A.** Yes, sir.
> **Q.** Look at that watch and see if you ever saw it before.
> **A.** Yes, sir. That is the watch I got where he told me to go and get it.

After it was established that Owens admitted he had hidden the watch under the barn, the prosecutor followed with more damning questions for Ragland:

> **Q.** Is that the watch?
> **A.** Yes, sir.
> **Q.** Did he tell you when he got that watch?
> **A.** I think he did. I don't recollect. To the best of my recollection I think he said he got it that night.
> **Q.** Did you show the watch to him after you got it?
> **A.** No, sir. I turned it over to the sheriff.

Another witness would confirm the ownership of the watch. Dave Montgomery, one of Hugh's brothers, testified for the prosecution.

Q. When did he leave home before his death?
A. Wednesday before Saturday the 16th of November.
Q. When did you next see him?
A. November the 17th.
Q. What was the condition of his body?
A. It was burned almost beyond recognition, but I recognized it.
Q. It was your brother's remains?
A. Yes, sir.
Q. Would you know his watch if you were to see it?
A. Yes, sir.
Q. Have you seen it since the killing?
A. Yes, sir. The sheriff gave it to me.
Q. Look at that watch and tell the jury what watch that is.
A. That is his.
Q. Tell the jury when you last saw it before he was killed.
A. He had it on when he left home.

Another crucial link needed to be established. Lester had testified that he took George Mask's gun but that Whit Owens had provided the buckshot that killed the Montgomerys. Mask was called to the stand. He testified that the gun Lester had taken was loaded with No. 8 birdshot.

Q. Were you at home on the night the Montgomerys are alleged to have been killed?
A. No, sir.
Q. Did you have a gun?
A. Yes, sir. A breech loading shotgun #12.
Q. Tell the jury what kind of shells you had at your house for that gun?
A. As well as I remember I had #8 birdshot.
Q. When had you used that gun before that night?
A. About three weeks before, maybe longer. I don't remember exactly.
Q. What did you use it for last?
A. Bird hunting.
Q. Was it loaded?
A. I couldn't say whether I left it loaded or not.
Q. If you did leave it loaded, what size shot were in it?
A. No. 8's.

Will Mathis refused to testify against his father-in-law, but he did admit that Lester had delivered Owens' message to him about killing the officers.

When the State rested, the Defense had their opportunity to call witnesses. Neither Whit Owens nor his family testified in the case, which is what defense lawyers usually advise, lest a prosecutor trip them up during cross-examination and force them to make damning admissions.

Instead, Judge Stephens, counsel for the Defense, asked to introduce a witness to testify that he had heard Lester contradicting the testimony he'd given in the Mathis case that Owens had given Lester the shells and said "kill the officers." The court ruled that a conversation held by Lester and other parties since his trial testimony could not be introduced but that the Defense could use the material if it gave the State the right to cross-examine him on the point. Given this condition, Judge Stephens declined to call the witness and entered an objection to the court's ruling.

Once the witnesses were presented, C. L. Sivley gave the closing argument for the State, followed by Hubert Stephens and his father, Judge Z. M. Stephens, for the Defense. Finally, District Attorney Roane had the last word for the prosecution. The jury received the case at 5:35 p.m., then retired around 6:00. At 11:30 on the morning of January 15, the jury stood eleven to one for hanging; however, they returned the verdict of guilty and fixed the punishment at life imprisonment. This surprising decision was later discovered to be a compromise: it was true that eleven members of the jury voted to hang the accused, but the remaining juror wanted to acquit him altogether.

The brisk pace at which the Montgomery murder trials had proceeded so far would be continued when the Bill Jackson case was called at the opening of court the next day. The day before had been consumed in securing yet another jury. District Attorney Roane, J. C. Wilson, and C. L. Sivley represented the prosecution, and J. H. Kimmons and J. E. Holmes the defense.

The first witness called for the State was Deputy United States Marshal Frank Matthews, who testified that he had sent John A. and Hugh Montgomery to arrest Will Mathis. Dan Welch and his wife, neighbors of Mathis, testified to finding the two charred bodies of the Montgomerys in the ashes of Mathis' burned house.

Edgar Welch, also a neighbor, testified that he had stopped at Mathis' house about dark on the evening of the killing and that Bill Jackson was still there after Welch left. Orlando Lester testified substantially the same as in his own case and at Mathis' trial. He stated that Mathis had shot Hugh Montgomery and that Bill Jackson had shot John A. Montgomery (which Lester had seen because he had taken the lamp into the room where the officers had gone to bed to get some corn cobs for stoppers to the bottles of whiskey).

Cordie Mathis was first called for the Defense, and she stated that Lester did the shooting. She swore that Jackson had left the premises before the Montgomerys went to bed. Her husband, when placed on the stand, also testified that Jackson had gone home before the shooting occurred.

Bill Jackson, the accused, then took the stand himself. He testified that he was over at Mathis' on the evening of the killing when the Montgomerys arrived. According to his statement, Mathis went off about dark and did not return before Jackson left for home, about 10 o'clock. He said he did not know where Mathis went. The peril of having the defendant appear on the stand was proven once again; as this retelling could so easily be shown to be false, the testimony was evidently more damaging to his case than any other testimony given. Jackson further stated that he arrived at home at 11 o'clock and that at about four o'clock the next morning Mathis called him to the gate, told him of the killings, and asked his advice about getting Shell and Jim Vines to give him an alibi.

The good citizens of the little university town were greeted on Friday, January 17, by an ominous headline in the *Oxford Eagle*: "In Shadow of Gallows." Then, "Whit Owens, Will Mathis and Orlando Lester To Hang on Friday, February 14th," followed by the longest lead: "While Bill Jackson Goes to the Penitentiary for Life and His Brother, George Jackson Will Have Two Years in Prison to Meditate Over the Crime of November 16th. Judge Lowrey Passed Sentence on Mathis and Lester Friday and on Owens Yesterday—A Solemn Scene in the Court Room When their Fate was Heard."

In another story in that issue of the paper, the leads were somewhat different—and far more accurate: "Three Were Convicted," followed by the subhead "Will Mathis and Orlando Lester to Hang, Whit Owens Receives a Life Sentence." A second subhead read, "The Case of Bill Jackson is now in Progress, and soon his Fate will be Known—The Taking of the Testimony will Begin this Morning—Whit Owens Arraigned for the Murder of Hugh Montgomery and will be Tried Friday for the Crime."

The closing arguments in the Bill Jackson case were begun Friday morning, and "splendid speeches were made by both prosecution and defense." It is unfortunate that transcripts of all the summations in all these cases have not survived. At five o'clock in the afternoon the case was given to the jury, who convened only for an hour before returning with the verdict of guilty. Yet enough doubt must have been cast on the case, because his penalty was not hanging but life imprisonment in the penitentiary, like Whit Owens'.

The trial of Bill Jackson was as short as that of Orlando Lester. All the witnesses agreed that he had been in the house early on the fatal night. In the end, Lester's testimony seems to have been the primary reason for Jackson's conviction. He had maintained in both his own trial and that of Mathis that Mathis and Jackson did the shooting. Months later, though, while standing under the rope that would strangle him, Lester would recant and say, "Bill Jackson is innocent of any crime." Will Mathis made the same affirmation at the gallows. Unfortunately, the jury did not have that testimony to consider back at Jackson's brief appearance at the bar of justice. Most likely, his only crime was being in the wrong place at the wrong time.

It was an impressive scene in court Friday afternoon when prisoners Will Mathis and Orlando Lester were brought in to receive their awful sentence. Judge P. H. Lowery told them that they had been found guilty of the murder of John A. Montgomery and set Friday, February 14, as the day they would both hang.

George Jackson, who was with Will Mathis when he was captured, pleaded guilty to being an accessory after the fact and was sentenced to two years in the Mississippi State Penitentiary.

When sentenced by Judge Lowery, Bill Jackson was asked what he had to say, and his response was, "You are sending an innocent man to life imprisonment." Jackson's wife and child, who had sat by him during the trial, did not go to the courtroom when he received his sentence.

As the *Oxford Eagle* article alluded, a second trial for Whit Owens, which had begun on January 11, would continue that same day. He, unlike Mathis and Lester, had not been sentenced to hang for the murder of John A. Montgomery, so he was tried for the murder of Hugh Montgomery as well. As with his first trial, it was difficult to empanel a jury. That process began on Saturday morning, and the entire day was taken up in selection. At the time court adjourned, only nine men had been selected. On the following Monday morning the voir dire was completed.

Added to the testimony introduced at his first trial, the State had further witnesses to prove that, while being taken to jail two days before, Owens, who was handcuffed to Lester, attempted to get Lester to refuse to testify against him, cautioning him not to say that Owens had anything to do with the shooting. Deputy Sheriff Ivy overheard Owens talking to Lester. In addition, Dr. A. C. Bramlett and John Hope testified to having heard a conversation between Owens and Lester on Saturday night when Owens spoke from the window of his cell to Lester at another window. This time the older man urged Lester not to tell whose gun the shooting was done with or that Owens had anything to do with the shooting. One person who would not testify against Owens was his son-in-law, who would say, "They tried to get me to go on the stand; I wouldn't do it; I couldn't afford to swear a lie for him and I would not swear his life away on account of my wife."

The defense introduced no testimony, and the State's evidence was the same as given in the trial the previous week, recounting how Owens had furnished the buckshot and told Mathis not to fail to kill the Montgomerys. As before, at the conclusion of the State's evidence the defense moved for peremptory instruction, but the motion was dismissed by the court.

The case was given to the jury Tuesday evening, and they brought in a verdict of guilty at noon Wednesday. Judge Lowrey thereupon sentenced Owens to be hanged on February 14. Most people following the trials closely thought Owens would take an appeal to the state Supreme Court.

The US attorney M. A. Montgomery reported to P. C. Knox, the attorney general in Washington, about what had happened in the Montgomerys' case. In part, he wrote:

> . . . There has been a very great deal of interest manifested in these cases from the very beginning down to this day— the people from this County and other Counties crowding the court-room every day for more than two weeks. And the tact and good management on the part of Judge Lowrey, presiding, and of the District Attorney for the State have been such as to win and deserve the applause of all good people in this County and in the State; and, in reviewing the proceedings from the beginning of the court to the end, notwithstanding the

excitement and the crowds, I do not recollect a single improper or unseemly thing that has occurred in any way in connection with the cases, either in the court-room or out of it. As I wrote you some time ago, it was very difficult to prevent a lynching, and an out-break of that kind was by many expected at any time; but law and order have been preserved. The members of the County bar, except those who were appointed by the Court to defend, have given their time free of charge to the State's District Attorney in every case, and substantial justice has been done.

I regret very much that things were put into such condition as to make it inexpedient at the last term of the Federal court to take up these cases, for if there ever was a time when it devolved upon the United States Court to show to the lawless element in the State that it has power to protect its own officers it was in this case; but, in as much as the parties had first been put in jail without bond by the Coroner's Jury to await the action of the State's Grand Jury, it was feared that this might complicate matters and unnecessarily delay the execution of the sentences by giving the attorneys for the defendants a right to claim, on an appeal to the Supreme Court of the United States, that the persons were within the jurisdiction of the State Court.

It has been a very heavy expense upon this County, but it has been cheerfully met, and the people are to be congratulated upon the result.

Justice for the dual murders had been served. Whit Owens was not finished yet, however. His lawyers would continue to file appeals that had to work their way through the system. In the end, the old moonshiner would prove more cunning than his younger partners.

Chapter Thirteen
Preparing for Hangings

As many gentlefolks in the community awaited the outcome of the various legal proceedings, most went on about their lives. January was a cold month, but it didn't curtail significant developments.

During the first week in January, Hal Ramey took the oath of office as US deputy marshal, to replace Hugh Montgomery. The talk around the federal building was that a better choice could not have been made. Later that same month, Ramey and Deputy Penitentiary Warden J. J. Henry took George and Bill Jackson to the penitentiary in Parchman one Friday morning.

In the meantime, Will Mathis had plenty of time to consider the doom that awaited him. If he had to die, he wanted to leave the world in what he considered a dignified fashion. The *Commercial Appeal* in Memphis was the first paper to report a request that he made. The headline of the story read "Color Line with a Vengeance."

> Much has been said and written about drawing the color line in the South, and the people of the North marvel that what to them seems a foolish sentiment should have such a hold on Southern people. They can not [sic] understand why it should be with us the ruling passion; nevertheless, it is so. It is not only the ruling passion in life, but it is a passion which is quite as strong in death. This assertion is amply proven by the request made of Judge Lowrey at Oxford, Miss., by Will Mathis, who is condemned to be hung with others at an early date. Among the number condemned to death for the murder of the Montgomery brothers* is a negro by the name

---

* This newspaper account is incorrect in identifying John and Hugh Montgomery as brothers. Any similar reports quoted hereafter are likewise mistaken.

of Orlando Lester, and desiring to keep the races separate in death, as well as in life, Mathis has requested that he be hung on a different day and from a different scaffold on which the negro culprit is to be executed.

This incident is not entirely destitute of some of the elements of absurdity; but it is quite a serious matter with Will Mathis and many others, and shows the intensity of feelings on the question of race separateness and the indestructibility of that feeling in this section of the country.

Other papers would comment about Mathis' request also. The *Clarksdale Challenge*, two counties west of Oxford, reported:

The man, notably the Lafayette county murderer, Mathis, who disapproves of the "social equality" that his hanging at the same time with his negro associate in crime would engender, is beginning to realize that it is never too late to mend. Had he exercised this delicately discriminating taste of his some months earlier there would have perhaps been no occasion for its development now. A hanging at best is a matter of the gravest import; but to hang with a negro, according to this hair-splitting reasoner, is adding insult to injury.

In their first Monday session in February, the board of supervisors ordered a public execution of Will Mathis, Whit Owens, and Orlando Lester. A committee of the faculty of the university had argued before the board in favor of a private hanging, but the supervisors were of the opinion that a better lesson would be taught by a public execution. The place selected for the execution was a mile southeast, near E. T. Buffaloe's place, where Steve Allen, a black man, had been hung a number of years before. The advantage of the place was that a crowd of any size could get in sight of the gallows. The Whit Owens case by then had been appealed, which would necessarily delay his hanging until April.

A great deal of interest was being manifested in the coming execution, and crowds were expected from all the surrounding counties. Inquiries were coming in from all over. Hotel rooms were being reserved rapidly, until the hotels were booked to full capacity. A projected ten thousand people would witness the final judgment of the murderers.

Despite Mathis' plea, the two hangings were scheduled to take place on the same scaffold and at the same time, on Friday, February 14, between the hours of 11:00 and 4:00.

As time marched on toward that date, however, the executions would be delayed. In the middle of February both Mathis and Lester followed the example of Owens and appealed their cases to the State Supreme Court. Mathis had previously stated that he would not go this route; he realized that the only good to be accomplished by an appeal would be to delay his execution, while the costs of the appeal would cost his wife all she possessed. As the execution date became imminent, though, the decision was taken out of his hands: "A few days before I was to hang my wife got enough money to appeal my case. My lawyer tried to get the record but the first lawyer I had never took a copy of the evidence."

By then Sheriff Harkins had made his preparations. The gallows had been erected and stood awaiting the time the higher courts would decide that its victims must pay the penalty for their crime. The opinion around town was that these appeals meant only a short delay.

The *Globe* reported that it understood most people were willing to be patient and let the higher court have its say, knowing that the prisoners were guilty beyond a doubt and that the gallows had been cheated only briefly. The paper did not think that any attempt would be made to lynch the prisoners.

Mathis' appeal was eventually filed—late in the afternoon of Thursday, February 13—by a lawyer from Water Valley named McGowan. Up to that point this attorney had not been a party in any way in the case, which increased the surprise and universal indignation in the community when his gesture became known. Some suspected that the appeal had been deliberately delayed until the last minute in order to give Mathis a chance to get rid of the main witness against him, Orlando Lester.

As for Lester, he had made no talk of appealing, but Professor T. H. Somerville, one of the attorneys appointed to defend him, took the appeal in his case that same Thursday. Thus the legal hanging scheduled for Friday was put on hold. Most of the town agreed that it was only fitting that he should appeal as the other two had done.

Yet Lester's appeal was not only submitted in consideration of fairness. No one thought it wise to hang Lester and thus remove the best witness that the State had against the other two, in the event that Mathis and Owens succeeded in winning new trials. C. E. Slough, the circuit court clerk, wrote a letter concerning the case to the State Supreme Court. It read:

> Hon. M. McClung:
> Dear Sir:
> In reply to your inquiry about the Lester case will give you an answer dictated by Lester's counsel, J. W. T. Falkner. The appeal in this case was taken simply to prevent the hanging of the negro until the other 2 cases were heard. We will not ask for a reversal but request you to see that his case is not disposed of until Mathis & Owens cases are affirmed. The negro is an important witness against the others as you will see from the records & hence the importance of holding back the execution until we see what the court does. Falkner & Somerville, Atty for Lester.

The public were not all so patient. They had been looking forward to a hanging, and if there was any chance a judge would let these villains off, a crowd of right-thinking citizens might have to come in and do the hanging themselves. In announcing the appeals, the *Oxford Eagle* included a call to refrain from such an outburst:

> It is with shame that we must admit that Mississippi has

the reputation abroad of having more lynchings than any State in the Union. However, it is but just to say that the difficulty experienced by the best citizens in upholding the law is the sole cause of the prevalence of lynch law. If such crimes as the murder and burning of the Montgomerys go unpunished, there is no need for our court house and we trust that no effort will be spared to bring about justice in this case.

This could well be taken as a none-too-veiled threat to the legal system and was probably regarded as such by the readers of the paper.

A sister paper, the *Commercial Dispatch* in Columbus, Mississippi, would be more fulsome while inveighing against mob violence:

> That Mississippi leads all other states in the number of lynchings that occurred in 1901 is a fact to be deplored, and in future prevented, if possible. Mob law is the next door neighbor to anarchy, and anarchy would displace all law. The occurrence of a lynching is drawing one step further away from internal peace and order, and opening the door for an influx of lawlessness and crime. It is no laughing matter, no matter about which to joke and gibe. It is the most serious problem confronting our people to-day.
>
> We would not say that the punishment visited upon the victim by mob violence is unmerited, but the result to the community—the shame entailed upon the community's regard for law and order—is without price, and is irremediable.
>
> The occasion for lynching is supposed to come from the laxity of the law—from long delays and sufficient prosecutions—but this is not the rule. As late incidents have gone to prove, in no state in the union are criminals brought to more speedy justice, or more sufficiently punished. The recent Montgomery murder trials in Lafayette County were the most complete refutation of this plea. The swift indictments and probably speedy trials of the murderers of Engineer G. M. Wray, on the Valley railroad, are affording another argument against it, in fact, the rule in Mississippi at this time, is for prompt trials of criminals, and as speedy dealing out of justice as is possible.
>
> It is quite in the line of reason that the increase in lynchings

results more from a bloodthirstiness that has been fed and flamed by immunity from punishment itself.

There was a time when the law was lax, when certain unnamable crimes, most hideous in the sight of men, were frequent and the punishment insufficient—and then mob law was the only resort.

The time is now ripe for the enforcement of the law against the mob itself. It will not do to have Mississippi at the head of the column of lynchings for another year. It is in the power of courts and the court officials to punish, and to prevent, by the wholesale application of legal remedies. And it is in the power of the law-and-order elements of our citizenship to diffuse throughout our state a knowledge of the evils of mob law, and abhorrence of its fearful results.

There is work for all in the prevention of its recurrence in every community.

They might have been thinking of a case in Aberdeen, a town eighty miles southeast of Oxford. On March 19 a large crowd gathered to witness the legal execution of Will Lanier at one o'clock in the afternoon. Perfect order prevailed throughout the affair. Lanier climbed the gallows for having murdered two brothers. He made a public address in which he stated that the cause of his downfall was gambling and illicit whiskey making. He had been convicted of the murders two years before, being assisted in the crime by two other members of his family, who were at that time in the penitentiary. When the rope stretched his neck, however, the spectators were horrified to see his head leap from his body, severed as completely as though cut with an ax.

Back in Oxford, the *Globe* commented on the delay of the inevitable caused by the appeals to the Supreme Court: "If the Supreme Court keeps this racket up of putting these trials off many more times, we are afraid they won't have any subjects to try. Patience ceases to be a virtue, don chu know."

Despite the delays, the Montgomerys were not being forgotten. In the second week in April a special citation was delivered at the meeting of the Sons of the Confederacy:

In Memoriam.

Worthy Commander: Your committee appointed to prepare a tribute to the memory of our late beloved comrade, John A. Montgomery, respectfully submit the following.

John A. Montgomery, at the age of 16 entered the Confederate service on April 1, 1861, at Fort Sumpter, S. C., and save when suffering from wounds, served continuously till the close of the war, surrendering with Gen. R. E. Lee, at Appamatox, in April, 1865. He took active part in engagements at Fort Sumpter, Bull Run, Groveton, Brandy Station, Fredericksburg, Fort Royal, Mine Run, Bristow Station, Chancellorsville, Wilderness, Spottsylvania, Jelico Ford, Gaines' Mill, Petersburg, Ream's Station, Hatcher's Run, Five Oaks, White Oak Road, Farmville, Cedar Mountain, and Appomatox. At Gaines' Mill, he was wounded three times; at Bull run, twice; on picket line, once in the neck; at Spottsylvania, once in the ear; at Jelico Ford, in the mouth and in the back; at White Oak Road, in the knee and in the hip; on a scout, once in the hip.

Let this simple recital of facts suffice for his military career, which has been rarely equaled in the annals of war.

Your committee deem it altogether unnecessary to attempt an extended biographical sketch of John A. Montgomery; yet it is a pleasing reflection that in all the walks of life, social and domestic, he was ever true and faithful. Finally, without entering into the horrible details of the brutal murder that brought him to his tragic fate, to be reminded that as an officer of the United States government he sacrificed his life in the discharge of patriotic duty may give us a ray of comfort to brighten the gloom of our sad bereavement. Therefore, be it

Resolved, That this Camp will ever cherish in grateful remembrance the name and fame of our departed comrade.

Finally in May, the Supreme Court affirmed the decision of the lower court in the Will Mathis case. The date for the hanging was fixed for June 24. The decision was handed down by Judge Calhoun, who stated that the case was unparalleled in the history of the state. He based his decision upon the confession of Mathis to George Jackson the morning following the murder.

Although the other two cases were to be heard soon

thereafter, people in Lafayette County were disappointed that a decision on all three cases had not come down. Still, general satisfaction was heard all around that the court made the right decision with Mathis and would likely do so in the Owens and Lester cases. As one paper said, "Our people have done the right thing all the way long—they have let the law take its course—but they don't want to wait always for the dastardly act of these three to be avenged."

Again, the not-so-subtle threat of a possible lynching. The people would prefer justice without too much delay.

A few days later, the *Jackson Evening News* would spread the word everyone in north Mississippi had been waiting for: "Orlandus Lester will drop to his death on the 24th of next month and answer the law for the murder of the Montgomery brothers in Oxford about a year ago."

In late May a reporter for the *Clarion-Ledger* visited Owens in his cell and had a short talk with the celebrated prisoner. Here is what he had to say:

> He is an interesting character study. Outward appearances would indicate that he was harmless and free from guile, but it requires only a few questions to develop the conviction that he is a man who could easily be guilty of the atrocious crime with which he is charged. . . .
>
> Owens is firmly convinced that he is going to secure a reversal of his case, but he is apparently not worrying over the matter. He was engaged in writing a letter to his wife when the reporter entered the jail, and the episode was devoted chiefly to family matters and incidental mention of his surroundings in the Jackson jail. His cell-mate is J. L. Leland, the safe-blower, and the latter was also engaged in writing. Owens remarked in apparent seriousness that he thought he had a nice gentleman for companionship during his stay in Jackson.

Around this time a rumor raced around Oxford that the prisoners had been spirited out of the jail and taken to an unknown location. This proved to be false, but it again emphasized how determined some were to see those men at the end of coiled ropes.

Within days, however, one part of that rumor would become a fact. Late Saturday night, Sheriff John Harkins was surprised when he received an order from Judge Lowrey, who telegraphed from Water Valley, to transport Whit Owens to Jackson for safekeeping. The order told him to take the southbound train and to secrete Owens out of town. The honorable judge had heard from some source, never disclosed, that Owens would likely be lynched by a mob.

The local papers were not at all happy with the judge's decision, arguing in print that Owens was as safe there from mob violence as he would be anywhere else. Furthermore:

> . . . our people have certainly done their part nicely in allowing the law to take its course in this horrible crime and they proposed to carry out this precedent they have set. The case, so we learn, has never been taken up by the supreme court, and it does seem that the Judge is carrying this matter a little too far. We appreciate his position as well as we appreciate his quick action in giving us a speedy trial in all these cases, but when that was done, it seems to us his work too should have ended, especially when there was absolutely no action here upon the people's part to mob him. Such actions will come nearer encouraging a mob than to have left him here, where he belongs, to meet his fate upon the gallows. This case has cost the people of this county dearly, and they are not satisfied with this unnecessary move.

Marvel Ramey Sisk would recollect that a mob actually stormed the jail. No doubt a crowd was gathered around the courthouse on that occasion, as they usually did, but no paper printed any copy about an attack on the jail. Ramey's daughter, however, would provide a lurid version of how Owens was hurried out of the county jail—only she had the state penitentiary at Parchman as the destination instead of the Jackson jail. She somehow omitted the role of Sheriff

Harkins in this clandestine move, but it is inconceivable that Pete Ramey would have made such a move except under the direction of his boss.

>On the night the mob stormed the jail Ben Markette, Linburn Cullen, and deputy sheriff Pete Ramey were among the many others who were trying to quiet the angry mob and keep the crowd away from the jail. But the situation began to look serious.
>
>Ben Markette felt a responsibility to save his client; Pete Ramey felt a responsibility to save his prisoner; so together they came up with a bold plan to try to escape with him.
>
>As deputy sheriff, Pete Ramey was permitted to enter the jail. He took Ben Markette and Linburn Cullen with him, and going to Whit Owens' cell, he handcuffed the prisoner to Ben Markette on one side, and Linburn Cullen on the other side. Quietly they went to the rear door of the jail. Just as Pete Ramey was ready to unlock and open it, Ben Markette shoved Whit Owens behind the door, put his own hat on Owens' head, then reached up and knocked out the light with his pistol. Under cover of darkness, and in a close huddle, the four men slipped through the door unobserved.
>
>"Pete," whispered Ben Markette, "if they recognize him and start to close in on us, I'm going to give him a pistol."
>
>In some alarm, Pete Ramey quickly objected. "By Joe, Ben! Don't you put a gun in the hands of that old fool; there's no telling who'll get shot."
>
>To carry out their plan they still had to cross the street in front of the jail, where the mob was milling and shouting. Skirting the edge of the crowd, they crossed over safely and made their way to a deep gully behind some buildings on the way to the depot. There they hid until just before day when a passenger train came through.
>
>They rode the train as far as Spraggins, a flag-stop between Oxford and Holly Springs, where they caught a ride (probably a wagon ride) to Como. Boarding another train, they took Whit Owens to the state penitentiary at Parchman for safe-keeping until time for his next trial. The mob had been outwitted.

This is a wonderful tale, but is probably just that. Given the order to move Owens to a secure place, Sheriff Harkins along with several deputies took Owens aboard the last southbound train and deposited the prisoner in Jackson about four o'clock the next morning. Owens came to rest behind the bars of one of the strong steel cages where murderers were usually kept, not Parchman—at least for the moment. In time he would get to see the penitentiary from the inside.

In retrospect, it is quite likely that Judge Lowrey anticipated the consequences that would follow a reversal of Owens' case by the Supreme Court. Enough murmurs of possible lynching had surfaced over the months to give the judge good cause to be concerned. Although no overt threats had been made, Lowrey might have felt that discretion should be the order of the day.

Despite his caution, the murders were receding in people's minds. As spring came on, so did the town's usual obsessions rise to the fore. On May 29, for instance, the *Globe* reminded the sports fans in the town that the Jefferson Military College baseball team would go against the University of Mississippi team the next Monday, Tuesday, and Wednesday in Oxford. According to the writer, "It is expected that our team will 'eat em up raw,' like they did the University. But they are coming 'loaded,' and good games are anticipated."

The issue of public baseball during the summer was on everyone's mind. The *Eagle* observed, "Is Oxford going to have a base ball [sic] team this summer? Not unless the town will promise to support one, and then we will have a good one. A good team here this summer would certainly help pass the summer days away. If this town will promise to come to the game every time and bring their clerks as all other towns do we could have the best summer team in the state."

The old bridge across the railroad between the town and the university campus made the news again in midsummer. The near burning of it the year before had likely not improved its dependability. In June a paper appeared suggesting that it was about time for the board of supervisors and the city fathers to demand a new bridge on University Street.

"Instead of building a new bridge, they patch it up every time it gets in a dangerous fix. Some day [sic] it will collapse and kill someone." At the same time the paper reminded the authorities of an old problem north of town: "It is said, and is a fact, that where Harrican creek crosses the public road between here and Abbeville is getting in a bad shape and needs attention. We hope that our supervisors will look into this at their next meeting." Before long before many folks in Oxford would be using that road to go up to Holly Springs for the retrial of Whit Owens.

The decision of the State Supreme Court to remand the case of Whit Owens back to the Circuit Court in Lafayette County had some peripheral effects. The question quickly occurred to many people that the hangings of Mathis and Lester antedated the new trial for Owens. While many wanted to see those two dead as soon as possible, others saw the need for keeping them alive. Hugh Montgomery's hometown paper, the *Pontotoc Sentinel*, weighed in with its view:

> Gov. Longino should turn a deaf ear to the efforts of Mathis and his friends to get a respite in his case for the purpose of availing the State of his testimony against Owens. Nobody would believe a thing he might say on the trial of Owens, and the probability is that he would not tell anything new, if he should be granted a lease of life. The execution should come off on the 24th according to schedule, and the world be rid of this monster.

Hardly were the copies of that issue of the paper distributed and read and spread under chicken roosts than word came to Sheriff Harkins from the office of the governor, granting Mathis and Lester a second respite and fixing the date of the hanging on September 10. Judge Lowrey and District Attorney Roane had decided to hold another special term of court to try Owens the second time. To convict him, they felt it was absolutely necessary to have the two condemned men's testimonies. A change of venue was also granted the

Defense, and the case was scheduled to be tried in Holly Springs on August 18. No one in Oxford was happy at these announcements.

The *Oxford Eagle* offered a reasonable and cogent explanation of the necessity for these moves:

> But there is another matter deserving consideration. If Mathis and Lester had been hung upon the day appointed by Judge Lowrey, there would be no evidence that would convict Whit Owens of aiding in and abetting the crime. From facts brought out during the trial in January, it is evident that Whit Owens was the instigator of the deed, and it is believed by many that his true connection with the crime has never been disclosed. Those who have the matter in charge believe that it is but right and just to defer the richly deserved punishment of Mathis and Lester until Owens can be meted out justice also, for, without the testimony of Mathis and Lester, there would be danger of having this arch schemer and leader in crime, turned loose upon our community again, in a few years, with his evil ways not improved by the trifling punishment of imprisonment. The delay of a few months cannot harm any one [sic], and a guilty man would probably go unpunished, and many might suffer in future years, by recklessly hastening the punishment which is certain to come in due time. We beg all interested in upholding the majesty of the law, to possess their souls in patience, as undue haste would cause one of the leaders in the crime to evade the penalty of his deed.

July was brutally hot, but that was not the primary cause of one Oxford citizen's illness. Seeing her husband being taken away to the state penitentiary for life had had a terrible impact on Bill Jackson's wife. She had become totally insane and had to be taken to the Lunatic Asylum in Jackson for treatment. Bill Jackson could only grieve for her from his cell. Later, in his petitions for a pardon, he would bring the extenuating circumstance to the governor's attention.

On the next to the last Sunday in July some people awoke to a great commotion. About five o'clock that morning Oxford's efficient night watchman, Linburn Cullen, shot "Scoon" Murphy, killing him instantly, in the street just behind the *Globe*'s office.

Cullen had heard Murphy, a negro, say that he was going to kill him and then leave for parts unknown Saturday night. The next morning Cullen met Murphy and asked him what he wanted to kill him for. The latter remarked that he was going to leave there and then grabbed Cullen's hand with his left hand, reaching for a brutal looking knife he had in his right hip pocket. He said, "I will cut your damned heart out." The *Globe* wrote "d—" as papers usually did.

> Mr. Cullen gerked his hand aloose from his assassin and pulled his pistol firing 3 shots and then 2 shots before his assailant fell. Mr. Cullen was given a trial before the mayor and a jury who acquitted him as he was perfectly justifiable. The negro was a bad character and was known as a "bully." The town has lost nothing and an officer has done his full duty.

If July was hot, August was hotter still, and some folks used the temperature as a reason to facilitate certain changes. Given that the sentiment against Whit Owens was extremely negative, more so after the Supreme Court sent the case back down to the county, it is not surprising that his defense team should want to spirit him out of the capital city. Thus one Monday when the temperature read one hundred degrees in the shade of the courthouse, Judge Stephens asked permission to take the prisoner to some cool place for a private consultation. The *Globe* was skeptical about the attorney's real motive:

> We don't think he found the cool place, but we would suggest that since he has gotten a change of venue to Holly Springs for his client, it was more to find a cool place than to get a fair trial. We think the ex-Judge had the Holly Springs ice factory in his mind's eye when he made the motion for a change of venue. A cool place or a change of venue won't save your

client, Judge, unless you have something more substantial in the way of direct evidence to offset the damaging array of proof showing his guilt.

On Saturday, August 16, Sheriff Harkins and several deputies took the train to Jackson and fetched Owens back to Oxford for the trial. One newspaper would report, "Hinds county's famous sheriff, Col. J. R. Harding, himself, brought Whit Owens from Jackson in order to avoid any danger of trouble."

The special term of the circuit court of Lafayette County, Mississippi, convened on Monday, August 18, called to try Whit Owens for complicity in the murders of John A. Montgomery, Judge Lowrey presiding.

Grand and petit juror selection consumed the morning until 11:15. After an adjournment until 2:00 that afternoon, Judge Stephens and his son made a motion for a continuance. The judge promptly denied it. Another motion was introduced, this one to effect a change of venue, accompanied by two affidavits. After some discussion the motion was granted, and the trial was set to begin in Holly Springs on Tuesday, August 26. This time around, Owens was represented as before by Stephens and his son H. D., with the addition to the defense team of ex-Senator Sullivan. Prosecution was in the hands of District Attorney Roane, C. L. Sivley, and federal District Attorney M. A. Montgomery.

It was variously reported that Owens looked quite happy with this first victory for his side, but his visions of freedom vaporized as the grand jury filed into court and announced that they had found an indictment against him for the murder of one Hamp Williams and the wounding of Walter Jones at a picnic east of town the previous October. The two had been shot from ambush, and the prosecution confidently claimed it could prove that Owens and Orlando Lester fired the fatal shots. That was the case in which Williams was not the intended target; but, unfortunately for him, he was directly behind Walter Jones, who had testified against Owens, Mathis, and Lester in another case. The bullet fired only wounded the intended victim and then struck Hamp Williams, causing his death. So after Owens traveled to Holly Springs to be tried in the Montgomerys' deaths, yet another trial awaited him.

At nine o'clock Tuesday morning, August 19, Owens was arraigned on the new indictment, and he pleaded not guilty. The court appointed J. E. Holmes and H. D. Stephens to defend Owens in this case. Those barristers immediately made a motion for a continuance, which was overruled at once. Then they moved for a change of venue, which the State and defense argued until 5:30 in the evening, when Judge Lowrey refused to grant the request and ordered the attorneys to proceed. A special venire of fifty men was drawn, returnable the next morning, when the case would go to trial. As in other cases concerning Owens, the prosecutors were Roane, Sivley, and Montgomery.

At that juncture in his life, Whit Owens stood as the accused of three different murders, one of which he would answer for the next day, the other two to be answered in Holly Springs one week later.

Chapter Fourteen
Owens and a New Venue

Legal action for Whit Owens' involvement in the murders of the Montgomerys was resumed Friday morning, August 29, in Holly Springs with a retrial for John's death. Interest in the case was unabated, and once again the courthouse was packed.

Ellen Welch was called as the first witness for the State. In this testimony she recalled hearing two "heavy" shots fired between nine and ten o'clock the night of the murders, November 16, and then two more about two o'clock. These times did not square with her memory at the Mathis trial. At about two o'clock she saw lights in the direction of the Mathis house accompanied by pistol shots. That was another piece of conflicting evidence. The next morning she and her husband discovered the other house occupied by the two smoldering bodies.

Orlando Lester testified that he had lived with Whit Owens for two and a half years. He recounted Bill Jackson showing up at the Mathis place, as well as Edgar Welch, who did not dismount and soon rode away. Among the details of his testimony was information damning to Owens. According to Lester, when he took the shotgun from George Mask's house over to Owens' house, Owens asked what kind of shells were in it, opened it, and then went inside and returned with some different shells. He told Lester he could not accompany him.

Under cross-examination, Lester was reminded of the many versions of the murder he had already told. Lester pointed out that this was the first time he had admitted to doing the actual shooting. He denied having told attorney Z. M. Stephens and others that Owens had told him to "put that mule up and behave yourself, and have nothing to do with it." He admitted that he was drunk that night, had drunk about a quart of whiskey, but that he knew what he was doing.

The next witness for the State was Will Mathis, who had refused to testify against his father-in-law in his earlier trial. He stated that when the officers came to arrest him, Orlando Lester had skipped out, fearing they were after him. He returned about nine o'clock and told him that Owens said for him to kill those men. Mathis was to tell the people that somebody had tried to kill him and made a mistake and killed the officers instead, since everybody knew that Mathis did not have a shotgun. He stated that Lester killed the men. After the killing, when the three of them went to Owens' house, Owens confirmed the message that Lester had brought Mathis to kill the officers.

Mathis then produced an unsigned note which he stated was from Whit Owens, sent to him while in jail, which read as follows: "Will, you tell them that you gave the negro the shot and that I had nothing to do with it. It won't make it any worse on you."

Mathis identified it as Owens' handwriting. He talked so rapidly and in such a low tone that his words were rarely audible beyond the fringe of attorneys.

On cross-examination, Mathis stated that he knew of no promises made to Lester or himself of life sentences if they would involve Whit Owens in the murder. Judge Stephens had the following exchange with Mathis, one that would be more or less repeated with Orlando Lester and various officials from Lafayette County and the US Attorney's office, all of whom confirmed what Mathis claimed:

> **Q.** Do you know whether or not any promise has been made to Orlando Lester that he would testify against Mr. Owens in this case, that his sentence would be changed to imprisonment in the penitentiary for life?
> **A.** No, sir. I don't know anything about it.

Q. You never heard of it before?
A. No, sir.
Q. You never heard of any promise being made to you about commuting your sentence?
A. No, sir. And it has not been made.
Q. Look at this letter and say if you have ever seen that before and who wrote it. Is that your handwriting? Now first, please, answer if that is your handwriting, without reading it all?
A. Let me read the whole letter.
Q. Can't you tell whether it is your handwriting without reading the whole letter?
A. No, sir. This is not my handwriting.
Q. You are certain of that?
A. Yes, sir.
Q. Say if you didn't say this and write this: "They said if I would swear against you [Owens] they would try to get the Government to pardon me and give me a lifetime in the pen. I told them I didn't know anything to hurt you. They have done Orlando the same way. They said if they didn't hang you a mob would come and take all of us out and hang and burn us, tried to make me swear it that way. They are going to keep Orlanda to swear against you in your next trial." Did you say that?
A. No, sir.

All during this part of the testimony, Mathis showed much agitation. He went on to deny that he had helped to burn the bodies, claiming that he was in the back lot catching a horse. He supposed that he had at first taken the whole blame on himself in order to protect his wife, as he heard she might be mobbed also, but that had been a false statement. He said that Lester had come to his house to kill the officers, and he prevented him. Subsequently, he was holding the lamp for the officers to go to bed when Lester came to the door and shot them. Mathis did not have his pistol; it was on the bureau.

When Lester returned after running off from the officers, Mathis said he thought that it was someone after the hog they had been dressing and shot at him. Lester made himself known and stated that he had come on Owens' orders to kill the officers. He showed the shells to Mrs. Mathis as evidence that her father had sent him. Mathis said he took the gun from Lester and told him not to trouble the men. He stated that they would not have been killed had not the altercation over the pistol taken place between himself and Hugh Montgomery. He protested that if he had wanted to kill them, he could have shot them as they rode up, or arranged to have it done on the way to town.

The State rested its case in the Whit Owens trial at ten o'clock Saturday morning, and testimony for the defense began. The Defense would rely largely on conflicting stories told by Mathis and Lester in the early trials, and their differing statements as to who killed the officers. Yet the damaging fact remained that Lester had in all the trials, save perhaps one, stuck to the version that he got the shells from Whit Owens, who knew for what purpose they were to be used.

This damning charge was further strengthened after the star witnesses for the State, Mathis and Lester, concluded their testimony. The next two witnesses, John Hope and Dr. A. C. Bramlett, were introduced late Friday evening.

The two men had overheard Owens ordering Lester not to tell from whom he got the gun and the shells. John Hope testified as follows:

Q. Where do you live?
A. In Oxford here.
Q. What street do you live on?
A. North Street.
Q. In going home do you go by the jail from your place of business?
A. Yes, sir.
Q. Tell the jury whether you heard a conversation last Saturday night at the jail between the defendant Whit Owens and anyone else. If so, tell how you heard it and what was said?
A. I heard some parties talking up there in the jail but I couldn't see them.

Q. Where were they?
A. I think they were in the two northwest cells is where I located them at the two outside windows.

The county jail was located on a lot just north of the Oxford town square. A plank sidewalk ran across its front side. Facing west, the two-story jail had cells on the north and south sides of the second floor, four to a side. According to John Hope, Dr. Bramlett, and later Sheriff Harkins, Orlando Lester was held in the northwest front cell, Whit Owens was in the cell next to his, and Will Mathis was in the next cell to Owens. Harkins testified that no one could communicate through the walls or via the hallways, since deputies had been posted there to prevent the prisoners from talking. Thus, they could only communicate through the outside windows. The guards at the time in question were the son of Tom Ragland, the jailer, a fellow named McClellan, and Marvin Moore. John Hope continued with his testimony:

Q. Tell the jury whether or not you recognized anybody's voice.
A. I took it to be Mr. Owens'.
Q. How long have you known him?
A. Ten or fifteen years.
Q. Where were the voices you heard?
A. He was speaking out of the second window and the other party was at the first window.
Q. Tell the jury what you heard them say?
A. The first thing I heard him [Owens] say, he asked him [Lester] if he told anything on him that evening. He told him he didn't. He says, "Well, don't never do it." And he said he wouldn't tell anything. And he [Owens] asked him [Lester] had he ever told whose gun it was and he told him he had not, and he [Owens] asked him if they hadn't been inquiring of him [Lester] whose gun it was, and he said they had. And he [Owens] said Dick Oliver has been after you more than anyone else, hasn't he? And he told him yes. Then he [Lester] told him the reason Dick was mad at him was because Dick wanted to

whip a negro he had and he [Lester] wouldn't let him do it and he had been mad at him ever since.

Q. Tell what he finally said.

A. I don't know exactly how it finally wound up. He told him not to fail to stay with him. I don't know whether that was just before or just after he was talking about Dick.

Q. Who was with you, if anyone?

A. Dr. Bramlett came up and I whispered to him to come up easy and let us hear what they had to say. And he stood there with me until they quit talking.

Called next to the stand as a witness for the State, Dr. Bramlett corroborated this story.

Q. Were you up near the jail last Saturday night with Mr. Hope and did you hear a conversation up there between some parties?

A. Yes, sir.

Q. Between 8 and 9 o'clock?

A. Yes, sir.

Q. Tell the jury what you heard of it?

A. The part I heard, there were two parties talking from the windows of the jail upstairs.

I don't know who they were. I didn't know the voices of either of the men. That is, I couldn't recognize either party. I heard one of the men ask the other if he ever told whose gun it was and he said "No." And he said, "Well, don't ever tell. Don't give that away." And after that he said Oliver was trying to pump him and find out all about the murder he could because that Oliver was mad at him in that he had a negro once employed and Oliver wanted to give the negro a thrashing and he protected him. He says, "That is the reason why he is trying to pump you to find out all about it."

Q. Can you tell whether it was a white man or a negro talking?

A. I thought one of them was a negro.

Q. How long have you known Whit Owens?

A. I don't know him at all.

That Owens feared he would be linked to the murders

received support from a different source as well. Circuit Clerk Slough came onto the stand to say that he had talked with Owens as they rode to Oxford the morning after the murder. Slough testified that Owens was ill at ease and worried.

His evasiveness was shown also in the testimony of Dan Welch. He said that Owens, when sent for to identify the bodies, denied all knowledge of them. While he played dumb on some questions, though, Owens was perfectly willing to answer others. Welch added a further detail that explained why neither he nor his wife had stirred from their house the night of the killings. He said he knew well the dangerous character of his neighbors, and though he heard the fatal shots and saw the light from the burning house, he was not going to venture abroad on such an unusual night. He was safest staying right in his own house.

The first witness called Saturday morning was Dr. Young of Oxford. A physician for thirty-two years, he had made the postmortem examination of the body of John A. Montgomery. Dan Welch and his neighbor had doused the fire on the bodies and then drove John's body to Oxford, while Hugh Montgomery's body was transported to Pontotoc. The postmortem took place in the witness room of the courthouse, a corner room on the second floor. It occurred two or three days after the murder (Monday or Tuesday, the doctor could not recall which). He described the mutilated condition and wounds of the body: "Beginning with the head the face was all gone except a little of the skull and all of the face except the lower jaw. The flesh from the left arm, beginning about two inches below the shoulder and extending down over six inches, was gone and the bone cut in two as if by a sharp instrument about three inches below the shoulder. Both legs were off about four or six inches below the body."

Young found in the body of John Montgomery masticated and undigested bread in the stomach and crumbs in the swallow, and he described the wound penetrating the liver and wall of the stomach. However, he could not tell which was the entrance and exit of the missile, as all external openings were too much burned to show.

Cross-examined, Dr. Young would say from the size of the wound that it was from a shotgun charged with large shot.

>**Q.** In your judgment was it a ball or a charge of shot?
>**A.** A charge. The indication pointed to a large shot. I wouldn't swear to that, however. We didn't find any shots in the body.
>**Q.** Did you know John A. Montgomery?
>**A.** Yes, sir.
>**Q.** Shooting a man of his size with bird shot, what kind of a wound would it make?
>**A.** It would depend on the proximity. A charge of birdshot, after passing from three to five feet from the muzzle of the gun, begins to scatter. It may tear a hole but some of the shot will strike the substance around the hole at that distance.

Tom Ragland, the jailer at Oxford, identified the watch taken from Hugh Montgomery the night of the murder and said that Owens had told him where to find it in his barn because he put it there. For this trial he added more details as to how specific Owens' directions had been. Though Owens was here being charged for the murder of John Montgomery and not Hugh, this testimony proved Owens' knowledge of and involvement in the fatal night's events.

>**Q.** With reference to a statement Whit Owens made to you in regard to the watch which he said belonged to Hugh Montgomery, tell the jury what he stated and the result of that statement?
>**A.** He told me where it was and how to get it.
>**Q.** Tell the jury what he said to you.
>**A.** He told me to go to his barn and go in on the east side, to go on until I struck the crib on the north side and when I got to the east side of a crib to go on north under it until I struck the middle pillow and dig down by the side of that until I struck the watch which was about six inches under the ground.

Q. Who did he say put it there?
A. He said he did it.
Q. Who went with you?
A. Dick Oliver.
Q. Was it at the place he designated?
A. Right exactly.
Q. How high was the barn from the ground?
A. Eighteen inches.
Q. How far was it under the edge of the crib?
A. Right at the middle pillow.
Q. What kind of watch?
A. An old fashioned gold watch.
Q. Look at that watch and see if you recognize it?
A. Yes, sir. That is the watch.
Q. How long had Whit Owens been in jail when he told you about the watch?
A. I put him in jail Monday and he told me about it Thursday and I went and found it Friday.

The witness also specified the location of the prisoner in the jail when John Hope and Dr. Bramlett overheard the conversation between Owens and Lester.

Dave Montgomery, brother of one of the murdered men, once again identified the watch as his brother's.

W. F. Ivy, a guard during the previous trial of Owens, testified that as Owens and Lester were going up the steps into the jail, handcuffed together, Owens said, "Don't tell about me shooting."

A. L. Wates, a prisoner in the Lafayette County jail, testified to having overheard a conversation between Owens and a Jule Elliott, in which Owens offered to make it all right if Elliott would swear that Lester had not come to his house and got the shells. Wates also stated that Owens tried to get him to testify on his behalf, promising to make it all right.

Dan Welch testified that he went over to the burned house before the bodies were removed and that Whit Owens was sent for to determine if the bodies were those of Mathis and

Lester, or Mathis and his wife. Owens replied that they were not, that his daughter and Lester were at his house and Mathis had gone home with Bill Jackson; he did not know whose bodies they were.

When cross-examined, Welch said that he had appeared as a witness in one other trial but had not testified about Owens before, as he was not questioned. The matter had slipped his memory until all of the trials were over and it occurred to him while discussing the case with acquaintances.

Re-examined by the State, Dan Welch said the reason for his family's uneasiness and their not investigating the cause of the shooting and unusual light was that he had been that evening summoned by the Montgomerys as a witness against Will Mathis in the case for which the officers were to arrest him on that fatal night. With that, the State rested.

The Defense introduced C. E. Slough, circuit clerk of Lafayette County, who stated that Welch had testified only in the Bill Jackson trial and none of the others.

Cross-examined by the State, the witness said that he saw Owens the morning after the killing. Owens told him that Cordie Mathis, her little boy, and Orlando Lester had come to his house between sundown and dark the evening before and that Mathis had gone in the evening to Dutch Bend, several miles away. Upon being asked who the bodies were, he said he did not know. Owens appeared very much troubled about something, Slough testified. He also said that Mathis' gun had been at his house for about two weeks; he had borrowed it to kill hawks. When the prosecutor asked him about Owens' demeanor, Slough answered, "He told me that morning he was sick the night before and had not slept any. I remember his stopping on one side of the road once, and him getting out of the buggy and I waited for him."

J. T. Fuller, justice of the peace in the district where the murder had occurred, was next introduced. A black man had been killed in the neighborhood about ten days before the

Montgomery murder; this, of course, was the Hamp Williams case. After the investigation, Will Mathis had come over to Fuller's field and asked who the community was accusing of the killing, and if they had accused him.

Mathis told him of having bought a new box of buckshot shells and having a double-barreled shotgun. The exchange between Fuller and the defense lawyer is quite interesting because it suggests either that Will Mathis really was innocent of the Williams killing and capable of joking about it or was guilty and trying to throw investigators off the scent.

Q. Do you remember seeing Will Mathis about that time?
A. I saw him the second day after that, if I am not mistaken. The negro was killed on Tuesday evening and he came into the field where I was at work on Thursday.
Q. The killing of the negro you refer to was before the killing of the Montgomerys?
A. Yes, sir.
Q. About how long before?
A. I think as well as I can remember the negro was killed about the 6th of November. I ain't positive about that. Somewhere about that.
Q. State to the jury where you saw Will Mathis.
A. He rode into the field where I was at work, and he asked me if the negroes accused him of doing the killing, and he asked me who they accused, and I told him the negroes seemed like they didn't want to talk. Perfect mutes over there, and wouldn't tell. And he asked me did they accuse him, and I told him no, that they didn't say who.
Q. Was anything said about any buckshot shells?
Objection by State.
A. He said they had better not accuse him of that crime.
Objection sustained, to which the Defense excepted.
Q. If anything was said about any buckshot shells, state what was said about them.
A. He told me that he had a right brand new box. Said he had just bought a brand new box of buckshot shells.
Q. Was Mr. Walter Gay there?
A. Yes, sir.

Q. Did he have anything to say to Walter Gay specially?
A. No, sir. He was talking to the crowd. Four of us were there.

The matter of Mathis claiming to have shotgun shells muddied more than one trial. Of course, his claim in J. D. Fuller's field does not in and of itself prove that he had any, but this testimony gave the Owens defense team a useful wedge. The defense pressed the point.

A. I said the negro was shot with buckshot, and he said they better arrest him for it for he had some buckshot. He spoke about having a Winchester rifle, and I said he was shot with a shotgun.
Q. Didn't he say he didn't have a shotgun and never had one on his place?
A. No, sir. He said he had a double-barrel shotgun.
Q. Wasn't there some talk about arresting some boys around there because they had buckshot shells, and he said you had better arrest me because I have got some too?
A. No, sir. Not that I remember of.
Q. Wasn't there some discussion about whether there was such a thing as buckshot shells?
A. I knew very well they had buckshot shells, but I thought they had to buy the shells and load them.
Q. There was a discussion about that?
A. Yes, sir. I thought they bought the shells and loaded them, and he said, "No, you can buy them loaded," that he had a new box.

Shell Vines testified that he had seen Will Mathis at the house of his brother, Ken Vines, the morning after the killing, and that Mathis wanted him to swear an alibi for him, but that he had declined to do so. (Mathis had admitted this in his testimony.)

The Court adjourned at noon and reassembled at two o'clock.

A black neighbor, Henry Thompson, lived on Tom Harkins'

place (Harkins being a brother of the sheriff). Thompson testified that he knew the parties involved in the case and that in August 1901 he had heard Owens tell Orlando Lester that he would cut his throat if he went about Will Mathis' house again. The obedience shown by Lester to Mathis and Owens was remarkable, and there may well have been resentment on the older man's part because his black worker was so friendly with his son-in-law. The defense emphasized this exchange, noting bitterness as a possible motive for Owens' attempt to implicate Mathis in a messy murder case.

T. W. Avant was present at an interview in the Lafayette County courthouse between Attorney Z. M. Stephens and Orlando Lester, and he had heard Lester say that he got no shells from Owens, that he was drunk that night. According to him, Owens sent no message to Mathis about the killing. Plus, the gun in question belonged to George Mask.

W. D. Moore of Water Valley, who had until recently lived in Lafayette County, swore that he overheard Mathis ask Lester if he had told that Owens sent the shells; Mathis allegedly told Lester, "You know I got those shells at Toccapolo." Moore also had heard Mathis say Owens had nothing to do with the killing, that Lester did the killing.

When cross-examined by the State, Moore admitted he was a prisoner in a jam himself at the time. Owens had told him that he had gone down to Mathis' house after the killing. What followed did not bode well for Owens' defense.

Moore had heard Owens say he got Hugh Montgomery's watch and carried it to his house. At the scene of the murders, he saw the bodies of the Montgomerys on the bed, Hugh's body being on the front side of the bed. He had also heard Owens say that he carried clothes of his daughter and grandchild away from the Mathis home and several of the party carried a bed. The witness couldn't say definitely anything about the matter, although he admitted that he knew his testimony would be more damaging to Owens than to himself.

Late Tuesday afternoon, the jury in the Whit Owens case returned an "emasculated" verdict, according to the *Globe*: "We, the jury, find the defendant guilty and recommend him to the mercy of the Court." Whereupon the Court required the jury to retire and put their verdict in proper form. At seven o'clock they returned with a verdict, asking "that he be sent to the penitentiary for a term of years."

The judge and counsel for the State and Defense then interrogated each juror as to what he meant by the verdict. Each answered that he wanted the defendant sent to the penitentiary from anywhere from one to twenty years. All affirmed that they did not want him to be hanged or given a life sentence. The court had no power but to pronounce a life sentence. Besides, everyone present knew that the defense attorneys would move the next morning to have the verdict set aside. In the end, Owens was convicted of killing Hugh and John Montgomery, and he was given a life sentence in the penitentiary.

By the next day, "reliable sources" on the streets of Oxford reported that Mathis and Lester would in all probability be respited for a short while, in order to present their evidence in the case against Whit Owens for the murder of Hamp Williams, which would come up in Oxford the next Monday. The word also leaked that Owens' trial for the murder of Hugh Montgomery would not be tried in Holly Springs that term.

Thus did things stand at that juncture. Mathis and Lester were to die on the gallows, Bill Jackson and Whit Owens were to be sent to the penitentiary for life, and George Jackson was to enjoy prison life for two years. At week's end Acting Governor Harrison had as yet received no request to grant a further respite to Will Mathis and Orlando Lester, murderers of the Montgomery marshals, who were to be hanged at Oxford next Wednesday.

Mathis and Lester would be called upon to testify in the next trial of Whit Owens the following Monday morning.

Owens was scheduled to face the charge of the murder of Hamp Williams, and it was expected that the testimony of the condemned men would be concluded in time for the execution on Wednesday. Some trouble was anticipated in getting a jury, however, which might mean that the opening of the trial day could be delayed until Tuesday morning.

Acting Governor Harrison said that he would not grant a further respite unless the request was made in writing by the presiding judge and district attorney stating that was necessary for the Owens trial that their lives be prolonged a few days. Appeals from the attorneys for the defense would be useless, and the respite granted by Governor Longino three months before was only for the purpose of securing the testimony of the condemned men and not an indication that there were any grounds for possible gubernatorial clemency.

According to the reports received from Oxford, Mathis and Lester viewed their approaching execution quite calmly and said they would die gamely on the gallows.

On the evening of September 5, Governor Harrison received a letter from Circuit Judge Lowery and District Attorney Roane requesting that the sentences of Mathis and Lester be held up for two weeks. This request was made in order that the men might be used as witnesses for the state in the trial of Whit Owens for the murder of Hamp Williams.

His conditions for staying the execution met, Governor Harrison thereupon set Wednesday, September 24, as the day on which Will Mathis and Orlando Lester must hang. Considering that Mathis and Lester were originally to have been hanged on June 23, a local paper made a fairly mild comment about all these respites: "Now another respite is necessary on account of Whit Owens, and the men have lived just three months longer than the law intended that they should. It is believed that this will be the last respite that they will get and that on September 24th they will go to the gallows and pay the penalty for their crimes."

In addition, on September 10, the *Jackson Evening News* and other papers reminded people around the state that this was the day that the felons were to have been hanged, but for their respite from the acting governor. The writer observed that Lester and Mathis were feeling very good over their additional lease on life.

Even before the gavel sounded the start of court on the 15th, the fiscal consequences of these murders and their prosecution had been heralded around Mississippi: "According to figures just compiled, the cost of the Mathis-Owens-Lester-Jackson murder cases in Lafayette county has already reached the enormous sum of $12,000 and only one of the four men indicted has commenced his sentence." By the time the whole sorry affair was finished and the guilty had gotten their dubious payment, the cost would rise to more than $15,000, a tremendous sum in that time. The paper went on to make a plea for Bill Jackson, since it was likely that he had no role in the murders at all.

> An effort will be made, according to advices just received, to secure a pardon for William Jackson, who is now serving a life sentence for complicity in the murder.
> Jackson is exonerated by the confession of Mathis, in which little reliance is placed, but other evidence has been adduced to show that he did not actually participate in the slaughter of the Montgomery brothers, and only happened to be at the house of Mathis when the deed was committed. Jackson is a criminal of undoubted guilt, and has been indicted for counterfeiting and making moonshine whiskey, but many citizens feel that he should not suffer punishment for a crime of which he is not guilty, and if he is released it is believed that it will have some effect in restoring the reason of his wife, who has been confined in the insane hospital ever since the horrible tragedy.

The regular term of the circuit court convened in Oxford on Monday morning, September 15, with Judge Lowrey presiding and District Attorney Roane on hand for the State. Monday evening was devoted to securing the juries, after which the judge charged the grand jury, pointing out to them the law that applied to the case. One writer would observe of Owens, "Nemesis, it seems, is still on his trail, and he must now face the bar of justice a third time and fight for his life."

The case against Whit Owens for the alleged murder of Hamp Williams was convened Thursday morning. Owens had been brought down from Holly Springs two mornings before. This trial did not take long, as the case went to the jury late that same day. Yet the jury did not declare a verdict with the same speed. The *Memphis Commercial Appeal* would report in a special from Oxford, "Although given the case last night, the Whit Owens jury has not yet been able to agree upon a verdict, and the impression is growing that a mistrial will be the outcome of the first effort to convict him of the murder of Hamp Williams, colored. It is understood the jury stand ten to two for conviction."

On the afternoon of September 19, however, the jury emerged and their foreman announced: "We, the jury, find the defendant guilty as charged in the indictment."

"Four times has a jury of his peers returned a verdict against the accused," read the *Commercial Appeal* on the 20th, "convicting him of aiding and abetting the taking of human life. Forty-eight men as grand jurors have indicted Owens in the cases and forty-eight men as petit jurors have sustained the indictment."

Few could have predicted that Owens would get yet another remand from the high court in Jackson and be retried in Holly Springs the following March. At that time, perhaps because Lester and Mathis were no longer alive to take the witness stand or perhaps because people were simply tiring of the matter, Owens was acquitted of the murder of John Montgomery. He was never again tried for the murder of Hugh Montgomery.

One of the memories of Judge Z. M. Stephens' family sheds some light on this last case. Although no one in the family could recall the particular case, they do remember a case that bears many similarities to the Owens saga. Here is the way one descendant tells it:

> I'm not sure of the year but Granddaddy hadn't been out of law school too long and he was in practice with Papa and they were trying a case over in Oxford. I think that the story was that this man had hid in some weeds at the end of a bridge and this fellow came riding across the bridge on his horse and he blew him off his horse with a shotgun. And I can't remember if I think Daddy told me that or if it is something I read in one of Faulkner's novels or if Faulkner wrote the story based on the true incident. I'm a little mixed up on that. The case had been tried before. The first time Papa lost it and he appealed to the Supreme Court and they found error and they reversed it. He had been sentenced to life in the penitentiary. The case was sent back and they tried it a second time and they convicted him again and sentenced him to life in the penitentiary and Papa appealed it to the Supreme Court and they reversed it again and sent it back for a new trial. Papa tried it the third time and they convicted him and this time they sentenced him to hang. And Papa appealed it to the Supreme Court and they found reversible error and sent it back for another trial. By this time Granddaddy had gotten out of law school and was with him in the courtroom and they were trying it for the 4th time and they were losing the case and Papa knew it. It came time to get up there and make the closing argument and Papa got up there in front of the jury and he swooned and fell out in the floor. They were pouring water on him and fanning him and they sent for a stretcher and they got him on the stretcher and they got him up about eye level with the jury and they were fixing to carry him out of the courtroom and he opened his eyes and he looked over at the jury and he said, "I know I'm dying and I've spent my last breath trying to free this innocent man. My young boy will just have to go on for me." And so he swooned again and they carried him out of the courtroom.
>
> Whoever was there that told Daddy about it said Granddaddy got up and he said he had on an alpaca coat—

whatever that is—and he said he let out a bellow like a bull and started making that closing argument to the jury. They had carried Papa across the street to the hotel and they had him on a bed and there was a crowd in there and he was—his eyes were closed and he was lying there still as death and the jury came back in and acquitted this man and so somebody came running from across the street to the courthouse to the hotel and came running in the room and told the news that the jury was in and they had acquitted him and Papa jumped up off the bed and grabbed his hat and went running over to the courthouse. Daddy said he asked Granddaddy one time if that story was true and he said Granddaddy said that's not exactly the way it happened but he never would say exactly what happened.

Owens had never been accused of any actual individual connection with a killing. He had not been tried as the man who did the killing but had four times faced a jury on the charge of instigating murder. The previous November, when a witness who was ready to tell the truth about Owens and Mathis was found, plans were formed to remove him. Owens, today's jury said, was the man who, using the dominated negro, Orlando Lester, as his tool, attempted to forever seal the lips of the witness, but when from ambush Lester fired the contents of a buckshot charge as he believed into Owens' enemy, he killed an innocent negro, Hamp Williams, by mistake. Williams, who was walking beyond the intended target, fell at the crack of the gun and died in a few minutes near the fire outside the building. George Dennis, who was near Williams when he was shot and killed, testified that he had been taken back to the scene the next morning by J. D. Fuller, Curdie Hall (who happened to be Hugh Montgomery's cousin), and a Sam Pon. He was then able to tell them how things had occurred and was able finally to locate his missing bottle (which he had bent down to look for right as Jones and Williams were shot).

It should be noted that a new wrinkle was introduced in the

trial of Owens in the Williams case. That was the testimony of two brothers of Will Mathis from Chickasaw County, where he hailed from. They said that Owens had tried to persuade them to do the killing because no one would ever suspect them.

Evidently, Owens wanted to get three blacks out of the way: Walter Jones, George Dennis, and Dennis' brother. Walker Mathis testified first:

Q. Tell the jury if you came to Oxford any time last summer and when it was, if you remember?
A. I came to Oxford last summer a year ago to see Will; it was when they had him in jail.
Q. Who came with you?
A. My brother Sam.
Q. Do you remember what time it was you came?
A. It was in August; I don't remember the day.
Q. How did you come from Chickasaw County?
A. I came by horseback.
Q. Did you see Whit Owens on that trip?
A. Yes, sir.
Q. Where did you see him?
A. We went to his house to get him to come to Oxford with me.
Q. State to the jury whether he said anything to you with reference to anybody, and if so what he said, and who he wanted killed?
A. That morning coming to Oxford he told me there were three negroes in this County down there that was meddling with them, or witnesses against Will, and said he wanted them got out of the way and wanted me and Sam to come up at night and said that he had men that would go with us to help kill them, and said that we could go back to his house and stay over the next day and leave at night. He said he would go to Oxford and he would be here and have Will in jail and there would be no suspicion about it.
Q. Do you know where on the road that was?
A. He brought it up two or three times that day, and the best recollection that I have one time was in the 5 mile bottom from Oxford. I am not positive but I think in the far edge of the

bottom where he brought the subject up, once.
Q. How many times did he bring it up that day?
A. Two or three times.
Q. Were you going to town or coming back?
A. We were coming this way I am talking about, and when we went to part at his house he said if we decided to do what he asked, to write him and let him know what time.
Q. What did you tell him?
A. I told him that was out of my line of business.

Called to testify, a Billy Coleman would remember seeing Owens with Mathis' brothers about eight miles east of Oxford on the Oxford-Houston road. He was in a field about fifteen feet from the road, beyond a hedge. Coleman swore that he heard Owens tell the two men something like "Come in at night and go out at night and you won't be suspicioned." He also noted that the boys were both riding mules while Owens was on a horse.

Another additional element in this trial concerned an apparent avowal by Will Mathis that cleared his father-in-law of any connection to the Hamp Williams murder. Judge Sullivan, Owens' lead counsel, put circuit clerk C. E. Slough on the stand. One of the issues that Sullivan took with him concerned missing documents, including several letters attributed to his client, Whit Owens. Documents had been transported from Oxford to Holly Springs for the trials but then had gone missing prior to this trial in Water Valley. The exact contents of the letters are not known, but the trial transcript leads to the conclusion that the defense team, including Sullivan, had the documents and misplaced them.

The district attorney objected to this line of inquiry, to which Sullivan replied, "I want to show, if the Court please, this: I want to show and prove by this witness and by three or four others that Will Mathis under oath stated that Whit Owens had nothing to do with the killing of Hamp Williams, that he loaded the gun himself, give it to Orlando Lester, and told him to kill him, and that we went and returned and said he had killed him, and later that it turned out that he had shot Hamp Williams, that he stated under oath in the trial there at Oxford, I want to ask that question of this witness."

The Court agreed to the question and Sullivan put it to the witness. "Now, Mr. Slough, did he not in this case in testifying there at Oxford when asked about that, say he was killed with George Mask's gun, and that he give him the gun?"

The witness said, "No, sir."

Sullivan continued to press the point, but Slough would not agree that Mathis had sworn to having given Lester the gun that killed Hamp Williams, thus letting Whit Owens off the hook.

Parenthetically, it should be noted that Sullivan grilled most of the officials from the Lafayette County trials with vigor, including John Harkins, the sheriff, and M. A. Montgomery, the U S district attorney. In particular, he made a strong effort to show a blood tie between Montgomery and the murdered marshals. Montgomery answered that they had tried at times to find if there was a connection but had never been able to do so. Sullivan suggested fairly bluntly that Montgomery had continued to evince an interest in the prosecution of Whit Owens that far exceeded his official duty.

In time, George Mask was called to the stand. Mask, age thirty-five, had known Owens for fifteen years and had married an Owens daughter eleven years before. His house was three-quarters of a mile north of the Owens place. He testified that Orlando Lester had borrowed his shotgun the day before the Hamp Williams attack, ostensibly to hunt for turkeys. He returned the gun the same night as the shooting at Boone School. The school was but three miles east of the Owens place.

This testimony was corroborated by Will Mathis and by three other men.

At last all of the evidence was presented, and the latest

jury spent two days in deliberation. It finally determined that Owens was guilty and must be executed. On Saturday morning Judge Lowrey pronounced the sentence "to be hanged by the neck until dead." The punishment set was the same as for Mathis and Lester.

Owens' attorneys at once filed an appeal with the Supreme Court, although the *Oxford Globe* noted, "It is believed to be useless by the bar here. They think that this verdict will not be reversed by the Supreme Court."

The *Commercial Appeal* agreed:

> Three times before Owens has been convicted since the horrible crime last November deprived Hugh and John A. Montgomery of their lives. The officers of the law have been as thoroughly convinced of Owen's guilt as have the four juries, and for this reason have they prevailed on the governor to stay the execution of Orlando Lester and Will Mathis until their evidence could again be given against the man they believe to be the most dangerous man of the gang.
>
> The opinion is freely expressed that if the law is not all technicality and fraud this conviction ought surely to stand, and rid the county and the State of a man so often declared a dangerous criminal.
>
> District Attorney Roane was freely congratulated when the jury's verdict was given.

Appeal Owens' legal team did, but the Supreme Court would take its time to act on that request. In the meantime the gallows still waited near Thompson Lake.

On September 22, Governor Longino announced that he would not grant a further respite to Will Mathis and Orlando Lester, thus clearing the way for them to be publicly hanged at Oxford that Wednesday morning. Hearing that news, thousands of visitors must have made plans to descend again on the little university town to watch the high drama of a double hanging.

The governor saw no necessity for a further respite. Both

men had given their testimony that resulted in the conviction of Whit Owens for the murder of Hamp Williams. The Owens case was under appeal, but the attorneys for the prosecution were confident that the Supreme Court would affirm the verdict, and they did not regard it necessary to keep Mathis and Lester alive in the unlikely case the higher tribunal might issue a reversal.

According to the latest news from Oxford, the condemned men remained in high spirits. They did not believe that they would be hanged Wednesday, feeling that yet another contingency would again save their necks from the halter. Lester had not finished writing his history of the crime for which he and Mathis were to pay with their lives.

Unfortunately for them, the last obstacle had been removed. No more stays would be granted. At last the community could witness the ultimate administration of justice, the execution of criminals who had so long been spared.

Chapter Fifteen
Father-in-Law Urges Suicide

Will Mathis had not been as sanguine as reported. The striking contrast between scheming murderer and devoted husband would emerge once again in a dramatic prelude to the final scene. On the Saturday morning before the execution, jailer Tom Ragland received an intimation that Mathis had received a quantity of morphine, with which he intended making away with himself when he found all hope of a respite was gone.

First thing Monday morning, two days before the scheduled hanging, Sheriff Harkins and deputies went to the county jail, cleaned up a spare cell, and then told Will Mathis they had a clean cell and bed for him across the hall. McGowan, his lawyer, wanted to talk to him in it, they said. Before he was escorted out, Mathis was ordered to strip. He was given a new set of clothes and sent off to his new cell.

After Mathis crossed the hall, a diligent search was instituted for morphine in his cell. Quickly they discovered, sticking in the bed post, two notes from Whit Owens. The officers went to examine every item in the room for the poison, without effect. They then turned their attention to Mathis' old clothes. After searching them thoroughly, the sheriff felt a package about the size of a piece of chewing gum in the waistband of the pants. Upon examination, it was found to be a nicely wrapped packet of morphine. Across the way Mathis then weakened and said the sheriff was the best searcher he ever saw.

He aimed to set the record straight. Owens had sent the morphine to him about eight months ago via a black prisoner named Walter Jones, who was allowed to roam freely in the jail corridor. He said Owens sent Mathis something to eat from his cell, and the morphine was hidden in the package. The reason he did not divulge this information was that he expected to take the morphine himself instead of being hung.

The notes from Whit Owens seemed to corroborate Mathis' story. First the law enforcement officials studied the signatures on the notes. Several of them were acquainted with his handwriting, and they readily identified that they were written by Owens. One peculiarity of spelling was especially pronounced. Owens invariably spelled the pronoun I as "Eye." That spelling appeared in these two notes; hence there was no doubt about their source. All of the officers around the courthouse were ready to swear the signatures on the notes were Owens'.

Though found after his trials, the additional evidence of these notes undeniably confirmed Owens' guilt in both the Montgomerys' and Williams' killings.

Following are exact copies of the two letters with peculiarity of orthography and diction. The first was written before any evidence of the Williams murder had been secured. No dates are given.

> Will, thay has been so miny lys swor on you eye dont think thay is eny chance for you and if you wil tel them that you give the nigor the shot & eye had nuthen to do wiv it, eye can com clear, dont you say anything more about Orlando killen that nigor, eye I am afrade he will give me away about it, Will eye dont want the godam raskal to hang you and if you want it eye will get mat [Owens' wife] to get som morfen and bring to you, old man Wintors and his hol famly eats it. She can get it there and yau can tak it and ease yourself. Your Fren- D. W. Owens.

That letter had been followed up by a note that accompanied the poison:

> Will, when you tak this rite a note an tel them you brot it in

here with you. Wil, put haf of this in somthin to ete and give it to Orlando. Eye hate to ask you to do this but eye am afrade he will tel ever thing he nos, be shore and do this. It wont hurt any worse. You neednt be fraide of going to hel, eye no they aint eny such place. Tar this up and put in yer slop bucket. Yor bes frin, D W Owens.

Why Mathis had not produced these notes in court the previous week is not known, but it can be safely ventured that he was afraid of losing his morphine. That would be a much more peaceful way to go than being jerked harshly by a rope around the neck.

Owens was penned in a nearby cell, and the sheriff marched over to it to demand whether Owens wrote the two letters and sent Mathis the morphine. Owens denied it emphatically. He said he knew nothing of it.

For his part, Mathis replied that he was a liar. He had sent it and he knew he sent it.

The reason for Owens' vigorous denials is not hard to fathom. These letters came closer to portraying the whole affair than anything yet discovered. They show that Owens kept on scheming even after he was behind bars. Seeing that Mathis was condemned to death, Owens tried to persuade him to poison Orlando Lester and that way remove the main witness against him. The trouble for Owens may have been that he wrote what he wanted done instead of talking his son-in-law into doing it.

After the discovery, Mathis completely collapsed. Now nothing separated him from the gallows.

Yet he would show surprising courtesy to those who had kept him captive for all these past months. On Tuesday morning Jailer Ragland was handed the following notes by the guards on watch:

Oxford, Miss., Sept. 24th, 1902.
Mr. tom Ragland & family, Dear friends it is today that I haf to part with you all that i rite you these few lines, thanking

you all for your kind treetment to me. i feal prepared to meet my God, & i hope you all will live a christian life & we will meet a gain where thire is no trouble but ever lasting life.
    your friend as ever, Will Mathis.

Whether by coincidence or not, Orlando Lester had written a very similar note the day before that:

> Oxford, Miss., this day the 23rd of Sept. 1902.
>   i was placed in this jail own the 17th of nov. 1901, and this i will say of the jailor Mr. T. D. Ragland, he is a good jailor. i can say nothing wrong of him he has treated me mity nice since i have been up hear and i highly appreciate all his kind favors to me and i truly hope there will come a time after tomorrow in a better world than this.
>   god bless all who reads these few lines or hear them read. may they all try and meet me in heaven. so good by. yours truly friend,
>   Orlando Lester.

The only bar to the upcoming hanging on Wednesday was the nagging question of whether the Supreme Court would grant one more respite for Mathis and Lester. Since by this late date that seemed unlikely, the Memphis paper took note of the very issue about which Mathis had petitioned months before:

> It will be an unusual spectacle when Will Mathis and Orlando Lester meet death on the gallows at Oxford, Miss., today, plunging simultaneously with the pulling of a single lever. Mathis is white, while his traveling companion to the future state is black, but they were co-laborers in the perpetration of a crime for which hanging is richly merited, hence no sympathy will be aroused for the white man because the color line has not been drawn in the plans for executing the mandate of justice. The event being unique, the *Commercial Appeal* will make an elaborate report of it accordingly.

Two other letters should be included in this sad record. During the early summer Will Mathis, thinking he was to die then, had written Cordie a farewell letter. Along with many other newspapers, the *Oxford Globe* printed it in its entirety:

>Will Mathis Writes His Wife.
>
>Below we publish a letter that Will Mathis wrote his wife several weeks ago. The letter states that he is being hung on the credit of some one else. Of course every one who has heard of this terrible affair has formed their opinion as to who did it and how it was done—and the prevailing opinion is that the truth has never been told. Yet they think Mathis is as deep in it as any one else. No doubt before this criminal is hung he will throw some light on the subject. The letter is as follows:
>
>Oxford, Miss., April 30, 1902—
>
>Mrs. Cordie Mathis: Dear Wife—
>
>It is while I can't do anything else that I take pleasure in answering your kind letter, received Wednesday. I was more than glad to hear that you all got there all right and are well. But sorry to find out that I have written anything to hurt your feelings.
>
>I have good hopes all the time and never believe that the people of Oxford would want to punish me if they knew the truth. It wouldn't be any trouble, I think, to convince them, but you know we would have to tell the whole truth to do me any good. But you have been too true and faithful for me to do anything against your will. Cordie, you may rest easy. I will go to my death before I will hurt anybody. You and Cleveland are so near to me it hurts me so bad to be taken from you for the deeds of others, and to think that they can run at large. You know all about the killing of the negroes.
>
>I knew nothing about it when it was done, but it was done on my credit. You know that John and Hugh Montgomery were not bothering any one but me, and if other people had attended their own business they would have been alive today, and I would have been with you and Cleveland, in place of being in this prison cell, sentenced to death.
>
>Cordie, rest easy about me telling anything on anybody else. I have never said anything that could be used in court and never will. I have lost all hope. All I ask of you is not to let any of those who caused this trouble raise my boy up to love them as a father. I had rather for him to come up as a slave under a step father than for them to raise him.

Well, Cordie, these are long and lonesome days for me. We are farther apart than we have been since we were married. Twenty miles is as far as I have ever been from you, and that was when I gave up at Dallas and you were here in jail. I don't wish I had killed anybody out there but I wish I had made them kill me instead of giving up and causing you to spend all you had on me. * * * I will close. This leaves me well.

Write soon. Your loving husband.
WILL MATHIS.

As of the 23rd, Governor Longino had received no request from Oxford to grant a further respite to Will Mathis and Orlando Lester; the next day, they would be hanged for the murders of John and Hugh Montgomery. The attorneys for the condemned men doubtless realized that further requests for clemency would be futile, and as they had no legal reasons why Mathis and Lester should not hang, or any desire on the part of the prosecution this time around to prolong their lives in order to secure further testimony against Whit Owens, the execution would take place as scheduled.

A telegram from the sheriff of Lafayette County stated that he had everything in readiness. The scaffold had been erected one mile south of the town at a point where the assembled thousands could get a good view of the gruesome event. The ropes had been thoroughly tested. All lay in readiness for the hour to take the condemned men from jail. The execution would take place at eleven o'clock.

Chapter Sixteen
Side by Side

A gray, damp morning greeted the residents of Oxford on Wednesday, September 24, 1902. Will Mathis likely saw the sun rise at 5:50 a.m. on a cloudy day; he would not see it set at 5:54 p.m. His life was shrinking by the minute.

Before his final march to doom, a *Commercial Appeal* writer was given permission to interview him. When the reporter and jailer reached Mathis' cell, the condemned man was speaking through the window bars to someone. Outside, crouched on the ground, could be seen the form of a woman, clothed all in black; by her side was a boy four years of age. They were holding their last conversation with their husband and father. A slow, drizzling rain was falling, and Cordie Mathis had wrapped her skirts about her and covered her face with her hands as she repeated several times: "Will, I can't hear you." As the reporter described:

> Her face did not show the sign of grief and suffering expected of her sisters in a higher sphere, but was strikingly pretty as seen today. Her perfect teeth, fine complexion and soulful brown eyes atone for all shortcomings in her dress and hat.
>
> Ever and anon she smiled and spoke to her boy, presenting a picture seldom seen among women of her class, but back of all her perfections was something that strikes one with a chill.

Cordie Mathis must have been an extremely beautiful woman because a number of reporters would go to great lengths to describe her, many without commenting on her social standing, as this Memphis reporter did. Another newspaper correspondent described the scene in similar, if richer, terms:

To the observer her bent figure was an exhibition of vivisection. Under the ravages of tragic imagination and the miserable realization of impending widowhood and desolation, she wept silently, caressing with her long, thin white fingers the bare head at her side. . . . Her eyes spoke the volumes that welled from her heart. From time to time she looked up at the cell with a wistful expression on her face, not despairing, not lachrymose, but patient and pitiful. She begged to see her husband for the last time. "Can't you hear me, Will?" she called through the distance. "Can't you see me?"

It was a cry of love, the call of an anguished heart to its recreant mate. She remained in the crouching attitude until she was led away by District Attorney Montgomery.

Perhaps one further description of her may be endured:

Mrs. Matthis is not unprepossessing in appearance. On the contrary she has many of the elements of beauty, although not molded in fashion's form or conversant with the ever changing styles and apparel of the feminine gender. But her brown eyes are lustrous and full of expression, her complexion is clear and beautiful, and her even white teeth show clearly behind perfectly formed lips of sensual redness. With the advantages of culture and fashion she could have been a reigning beauty. But the little woman who was soon to be made a widow by the stern edict of the law did not present fashionable appearance as she groveled on the ground within the shadow of the grim walls that kept her husband from liberty. She was slovenly clad in a faded black dress that had seen much wear, and covering her luxuriant brown hair was a poke sunbonnet.

The prisoner started slightly when the officer called his name and walked to the door. According to the reporter: "He had the look that comes from long confinement; his flesh being flabby, his eyes clear and his action nervous. He asserts that he has no fear." Mathis went back to the window and said, "Cordia, wait a minute."

Then he was ready for the interview. Little new information would emerge from this session, because Mathis merely repeated factors that were already known. Often he would start to make a statement and then break off to take up a new idea. He pointed out a tablet manuscript and said his story was within, but on being asked if only the truth was told there, he confessed, "No." In explanation he began to say something about telling the truth if it were not for causing his wife more trouble, and then broke off.

He requested its publication. "I am an innocent man, but would rather die for something I have not done than if I had done it. I am prepared to go. Cordia has always been a mighty true wife to me, and has stuck to me and been the best friend I've had. I want to say the Montgomerys were friends of mine, and I never enjoyed myself more than I did the night of the killing up to 10 o'clock."

Cordie added her part: "Will has been as true a husband to me as any man could have been to a wife. He always tried to make me enjoy myself. We had as happy a home as anybody could have had. He is not guilty of the crime he is charged with. It is mighty hard for me to give up such a good husband in this way, but it is good consolation that he is prepared to meet his God, where there will be no more sorrow. He leaves me and his sweet little boy, but there will be a day when we all will meet again."

A somber crowd, as many as 1,500 people, had kept a muted watch around the jail all night, though most of the thousands of execution spectators were still abed or would not arrive until morning, bringing with them their lunches and whiskey jugs and eagerness to watch two men die. How Will Mathis and Orlando Lester fared during the night is not clear.

One report said that Mathis spent a restless night and at frequent intervals could be heard in the cell. He was nervous and excited by the least approach by the guard.

Another claimed that he and Lester had retired early Tuesday night and slept well. Lester evidently had a better night. That evening a military band had given a concert at

The Thompson House, across from the Lafayette County jail, on the day of the hangings

the opera house and the music could be heard as far as the jail. Lester remarked to a guard that he loved music and that this would be the last he would ever hear. Then he rolled over and went back to sleep.

According to longstanding custom, the two men were offered whatever they wanted for their last meal. Mathis requested ham, biscuits, and coffee. Lester asked for fried chicken, with plenty of fat gravy, eggs, and coffee. Both were given what they requested and ate heartily, according to the guards. Neither asked for stimulants and none were given.

The day broke gloomy, and long before most citizens were awake the county jail was stirring and bustling. Jailer Ragland directed deputies in their duties until Sheriff John Harkins arrived at about eight o'clock. US District Attorney Montgomery visited each condemned man's cell to take their final statements. While he was at Mathis' cell, an earnest conversation occurred between the prosecutor and the criminal, the nature of which was not divulged. It is believed that he made a statement incriminating several parties in the moonshining and counterfeiting operations in the district where he formerly lived.

Whit Owens had already been removed from the premises. Early Tuesday morning Deputy Sheriff Pete Ramey had taken Owens on the northbound train to Holly Springs for safekeeping. While the authorities there could not refuse him asylum, the citizens residing near the jail were not pleased by the possibility of a raid by an angry mob. After all, this was Lafayette County's dance.

The crowd began to gather early in the morning. As the day got brighter, the crowd got bigger, noisier, and more restive. More than one gallon jug of moonshine passed hands. Some of the visitors from rural districts insisted on venturing inside the jail grounds but were beaten back by the determined deputies at the gate. One man became obstreperous and was immediately hustled inside to a cell to cool off. He did not get to witness the executions. As one deputy recalled, "Ribald and gruesome remarks were heard on all sides and there was enough blasphemy to shock even an old steamboat captain."

The square was black with people. Windows and verandas of the hotels were crowded as they had never been before in Oxford. The incoming trains emptied thousands of people into the small town. Men from the country came in with their wives and children. They brought corn for their horses and lunches for themselves. About the courthouse square and federal building the streets were lined with wagons. Teams were hitched in every available space. All roads led to the scene of execution. About the jail yard, armed deputies kept the crowd in order. Gun barrels gleamed, and the glitter of pistols peeped from the holsters of the gentlemen of the law.

People came from all walks of life. Schoolgirls, with books under their arms; men on horseback; boys with their faces in a pucker; men of grit; bullies with loud talk; sedate, conservative businessmen, and show folk: all mingled in a gathering that surged about the jail like the flotsam of an unruly tide.

The number of women of all classes who mingled with the throng was nothing short of astounding. They seemed roused by the same morbid curiosity as their male counterparts, and they jostled their neighbors just as energetically to obtain a good vantage point.

After their final statements were given, the two prisoners were dressed for their final public appearance. At nine o'clock Mathis was shaved in the corridor outside his cell by a black barber. His hands were securely bound with irons, and in the middle of the handcuffs was attached a stout rope which remained constantly in the hands of the turnkey. The precaution seemed unnecessary, but Mathis might have seized the razor and used it with deadly effect, even though his hands were manacled. He seemed in a state of total collapse. As he sat in a straight-back chair, he trembled constantly. An observer would later give this account of the shaving: "A radically wicked person is incapable of suffering anything but pain. Mathis, however, was more weak than wicked. He was actuated in what he did by Whit Owens, who is under sentence to hang next month."

Mathis was an ideal degenerate. Every feature emphasized it. His eyes, his mouth, his chin, his voice, his demeanor all clearly illustrated the pervert. He sat in the chair with his eyes wandering vacantly as he was shaved. All spectacles of wretchedness are distressing and there seemed to be a condoning misery in his heart for his wife and child that carried with it a lasting torment. "If it was not for my wife and little boy," he said, "I would not be afraid to die." He shook with emotion. "What will become of them?" he sighed. There was about him the tremor of internal turmoil, the desperate sense of loss showed itself, and his eyes indicated a growing conflict between stubborn self-will and a sickening apprehension. He was not defiant in the face of doom.

"All I have to say," said Mathis, as he was being prepared for the ordeal, "is that Bill Jackson is an innocent man, and for the sake of his poor wife, who is in the asylum, I hope he will be released from the penitentiary. He did not take any part in the killing and was not present when it occurred. This is the truth, and I am not afraid to assert it before God in whose presence I am soon to go. Bill Jackson was my friend and I want to see him released."

Casually he brought up another topic that no one was expecting. It involved one of a series of unsolved murders of black men that had taken place more than a decade ago. Now Mathis related the story that implicated his father-in-law, Whit Owens, and two cousins, Brice Owens and Charles "Charley" Owens. According to his account, a dozen years earlier a negro who was suspected of turning state's evidence against Whit Owens was enticed into a cypress swamp by the trio. Whit and Brice Owens held the victim's arms pinioned while Charley Owens slit his throat with a large knife.

A later search of the records verified the killing, but this was the first word ever given concerning the guilty parties. Shortly after the murders of the Montgomerys, Brice Owens had fled to Texas. Charley Owens was now dead.

Lester was in excellent spirits and had very little to say when a reporter called about 9:30. He said he had made his final preparations on Sunday and since then had calmly waited the time to arrive when he would pay the penalty for his part in the awful crime of November 16.

While he was talking, he held in one hand a bulky manuscript. Lester was occupied to the last moment with his life's history. More than seven hundred pages had been carefully ruled and written. It was the book he had written giving his version of the tragedy, and he intended for it to be published in volume form in one of the local newspapers.

Scattered about in the manuscript were a number of illustrations rudely drawn by Lester. The pictures purported to represent moonshine distilleries and the horses of revenue officers; and he was familiar with both, for the greater portion of his life had been spent among the illicit retailers in the neighborhood where Mathis lived.

A last letter to his mother was given to District Attorney Montgomery. In this he said he had not lived up to her teachings and prayed his mother to watch the other boys and keep them at home. To his sister he left his Bible, and to both he left his love and assurance that he would meet them in heaven.

Of the five men implicated in the murder of the Montgomerys—Whit Owens, Orlando Lester, Will Mathis, George Jackson, and Bill Jackson—Lester was unquestionably the most intelligent. He wrote in a legible hand, used fairly good English, and displayed wonderful shrewdness in answering questions. Although he was only twenty years of age, he was quick-witted, and the amazing manner in which he conflicted the evidence was the chief cause of the delay in the meting out of justice. His contradictory tales were not told without a purpose.

Sheriff Harkins had long before decided not to allow Cordie Mathis into her husband's cell on the last day for fear of a breakdown by husband or wife. Her grief, however, moved all the lawmen to sympathy, and she was permitted to pass upstairs to the cell and remain a few minutes with her condemned husband before she was led out.

Around ten o'clock the two men were visited by ministers. Half an hour later the Rev. R. G. Porter, the Methodist minister, left the jail. The Rev. N. W. P. Bacon had already visited Mathis on Tuesday afternoon and was back Wednesday morning, praying with him and striving to direct his attention and thoughts for death. Mathis listened respectfully, but to the last protested that he was innocent. Rev. Bacon stayed with his would-be convert all the way to the scaffold. Rev. A. W. Williams, pastor of the black Baptist Church, remained with Lester to the end.

At 11:15 a wagon with two black coffins passed, and the crowd became hushed. At 11:20, Sheriff Harkins and special guards arrived. An open farm wagon with four board seats, driven by Doak Matthews, who worked for the sheriff, drew up at the jail gate. It was the death cart, though "not of the fashion in which Du Barry rode to the guillotine, but ominous in its present mission," noted one reporter. It was the wagon of the condemned, and the final ride to death was about to begin. There was a movement of the crowd toward the courthouse.

Matthews' father, Mr. P. E. Matthews, the former sheriff who officiated at Lafayette County's last hanging, was in the rear seat. He had been asked to render advice and assistance during the function if necessary. Suddenly there was a hush in the hum and buzz of conversation and jest. Forms darkened the jail door, and a moment later the party came out.

It was exactly 11:55 when Sheriff Harkins and Jailer Ragland emerged bearing Will Mathis between them. The prisoner's hands were securely strapped behind his back and he walked with a quick, cat-like gait. Mathis had recovered his composure. Head bowed but body straight, he was dressed in a black coat, gray pants, no tie or cuffs, and only a bit of ribbon in his shirt showed color.

His hat was too large and dropped to his ears. It was of the exaggerated Texas cowboy pattern. His weak little eyes blinked in the sunshine. He was emaciated and colorless and already looked more like a corpse than a man, but he seemed to gain strength in the sunshine and walked firmly to the wagon, taking his place on the second seat.

Just in the rear came Deputy Sheriffs Pete Ramey and E. E. Temple escorting Lester, who bowed to right and left and addressed several acquaintances. Dressed in blue serge with a bow of blue ribbon in his buttonhole, he appeared more to be a bridegroom than a man walking in the shadow of death. They were followed by a posse of fifteen armed deputies carrying shotguns. The officers and prisoners climbed to the seats on the wagons, the officers mounted their horses, and the death march to the gallows was commenced.

The preacher turned Cordie's head as her husband rolled by them, but Clelon extended both arms to his father. Cordie remained at the jail the rest of the day, not leaving for Yocona until she knew the body had been released.

The crowd moved forward. It was a procession of death, spectacular in its awful silence. Not a word was spoken. Mayor Adams, Deputies Ramey, Avent, Anderson, and Constable Roach, mounted, formed the advance guard and, as out-riders for the death cart, headed the way to the scene of expiation. The wagon followed, twenty mounted deputies bringing up the rear.

Because of the crowd in the streets the cortege proceeded slowly around the public square. Immediately following the line of wagons and other vehicles was a multitude on foot who walked energetically to keep pace with the procession.

Just as the party was about to turn from the public square to South Street, the bell in the courthouse tower tolled the hour of twelve. Given the occasion, it sounded like a funeral knell for the condemned men, and it caused a hush among the marching assembly. Mathis and Lester were visibly startled by the solemn peals from the dome of the building behind them, though one report said that Mathis looked up at the clock and smiled. The procession and its motley escorts turned east on Lake Street.

Some women of Oxford viewed the mob from windows along the line of march, Kodaks flashing. Two women on horseback joined the van in a morbid desire to witness the fearful spectacle. Men and boys on foot scrambled and fell over each other as they trampled over a muddy, mucky road to see a white and black man die side by side.

The mile-long route from the jail to the gallows seemed much longer to many of the spectators. The scaffold had been erected in a natural amphitheater south of town in Thompson's Bottom, and the hillsides were already black with the assembled thousands packed closely together. The formation of the amphitheater was such, however, that all could obtain a good view without craning. A rope had been extended around the perimeter of the gallows, and armed deputies prevented any encroachment by the crowd. The newspaper correspondents who arrived were required to show their credentials before being permitted to enter in a small crowd.

Up on the hilltop extended a long line of carriages, buggies, carts, mules and even ox wagons used by the spectators as a means of transportation. A survey of the multitude from the platform of the gallows showed that it was comprised chiefly by country people, perhaps a third of the number being African American. The latter were very quiet and made no demonstrations.

Precise details about what happened when were confusing after the fact. Someone reported that Lester mounted the scaffold first; others said that the sheriff did. It makes sense that upon reaching the gallows Sheriff Harkins led the procession up the steps, followed by Jailer Ragland, who was holding Mathis. Deputy Pete Ramey followed with Lester. Reverends Bacon and Williams came next.

Mathis smiled as he stepped onto the scaffold and spoke to several persons whom he recognized. On reaching the top of the stage, Lester paused and calmly surveyed the sea of faces stretching out in every direction. His expression was placid and he betrayed no emotion. A reporter described the condemned men: "Matthis wore a light black coat, brown trousers, rough shoes, and a faded black slouch hat very much worse for wear. The negro was stylishly dressed in a dark blue suit and blue negligee shirt."

By 12:25 the party on the gallows was fully assembled.

From among the crowd came cries for Mathis and Lester to talk to them. Mathis, with his knee on the railing, responded at first that he had nothing to say, as he had told all he knew on the witness stand. He stepped back a few paces and Lester came forward.

"I don't care to make any statement," he said in reply to the clamor of the multitude for a speech.

"Well, tell us if you cut the legs off the Montgomerys the night of the killing," several persons requested.

"No, I didn't cut their legs off. They wasn't cut off that I know of."

"Who did the shooting?"

"I did the shooting."

"Was the house burned before you left?"

"Yes, Mathis set the house on fire and we left together."

"What part did Whit Owens take in the killing, and did you go to his house?"

"Yes, I went to Owens' house to get some shells, and told him what we intended to do. He urged me to do the killing, and told me to tell Mathis to kill them."

"Did Owens take part in the killing?"

"No, he was not there, but arrived afterwards and helped burn the bodies. Jackson was not there, either, when we killed them."

"Who told you to shoot them?"

"Will Mathis told me to shoot them, and said he would shoot me if I didn't."

While this impromptu interview was in progress, Mathis was holding a whispered consultation with the minister Bacon. At its conclusion the reverend came forward and said that Mathis had requested him to say that he had written a book telling all about the tragedy, which would be issued in printed form and sold for the benefit of his wife. Mathis asked that all his friends read the book and study well the moral lesson it contained.

Mathis was asked several questions by the crowd, all relating to details of the killing, and he answered with some hesitation. He admitted the genuineness of the letters received from Whit Owens containing the morphine that Owens urged to be used to kill Lester while in jail.

"I do want to say," added Mathis, "that Bill Jackson is an innocent man; and I hope you will all help get him out of the penitentiary where he has been placed by false witnesses."

Lester, still replying to questions, made the important statement that Cordie Mathis had urged her husband not to kill the men and that Bill Jackson had advised against it. Both men were asked if the bodies had been mutilated before burning, and both denied it.

Orlando Lester was more communicative. He seemed to understand that the eye of the crowd was centered upon him. He said that he had fired the two fatal shots.

"Where did you get your gun?"

"Whit Owens got it for me."

"Did he give you the shells?"

"Yes, sir."

"Did you cut their legs off?"

"No, sir, I did not see that done."

"Who cut the heads off?"

"I never saw any one cut the heads off. It wasn't done before I left."

"Did Owens know about the killing?"

"Yes, sir, I think he told Mr. Mathis to do it."

"Who set fire to the house?"

"Mr. Mathis."

"Did you fire the shots?"

"Yes, sir, I fired the shots. Mr. Mathis told me to, and I fired."

"Did he threaten you?"

"No, sir, he just told me to shoot, and I did. He held the lamp so I could see."

"Were both men in bed?"

"No, sir. Mr. John Montgomery was in bed, but Mr. Hugh Montgomery was just fixin to get in bed."

Mathis came forward as if to speak.

"Speak it out, Will," called someone. "Get it off your mind, old man. You are looking God in the face now."

"I know it, boys, and if I was not afraid for my wife and the boy I would tell it all, but I guess—"

"Go on, old man, tell it. We'll look after your wife and child."

"No, I guess I have said enough. There have been lots of lies told on me."

"Were those letters published in the *Commercial Appeal*, said to be written by Whit Owens, genuine?"

"Yes, he wrote them when he sent me the morphine. He wanted me to kill Orlando so he could not testify. Yes, they were his letters."

"When did he send you the morphine?"

"It was last February. He sent it by a negro named Walter Davis [Walter Jones]."

"Did Bill Jackson know about the killing?"

"No, he is entirely innocent, so help me God."

Someone called to Lester: "Orlando, is Mathis telling the truth?"

Lester advanced and raised his handcuffed wrists: "No, sir, he ain't. Bill Jackson was there. He had heard Owens tell Mathis to kill the Montgomerys. Mrs. Mathis was in the back room. She knew and told Mathis not to do it, as it was a bad thing. Bill Jackson said, 'She's right, Will, don't do it.' Mr. Jackson left to get bond for Mathis before the killing occurred."

This ended the talk on the scaffold. Lester's ability to speak to the crowd was worn out. He became nervous.

Feeling that time was being wasted by the people in idle questions, Sheriff Harkins made a motion to the questioners to desist. Reverend Bacon then asked, as the prisoners were about to be launched into eternity, that the people remove their hats and bow their heads reverently in prayer. Reverend Bacon made a fervent appeal for the souls of the two men at the mercy seat. He was followed by Rev. A. W. Williams, who offered a prayer for Lester.

Both men then requested the ministers to thank the people for their kind treatment. A final handshaking with the clergymen followed, and just as the black caps were about to be adjusted, David Rogers, a former deputy United States marshal, ascended the gallows and shook hands with Mathis.

"You've done some hard things against me, and I've done some hard things against you," said Mathis, "but we can forget and forgive them all now. I feel kindly toward you." Rogers then descended from the gallows.

"Some things have been put upon me that I didn't do," were the final words of Will Mathis, "and if I had told the whole truth I would be a free man today. I want my friends here to quit drinking and persuade others to quit. Whiskey will ruin any man. Good-bye to all of you."

Mathis and Lester shook hands with the officers, and the next instant the light of the world was shut out forever from their eyes as the officers deftly placed black caps over their heads. Jailer Ragland placed the cap over Lester's head at 12:47, and Mathis took his last look at the world at 12:49 before Sheriff Harkins performed the like function. The straps were tightened, causing both to visibly wince. In the next instant the nooses were fitted around their necks, and they stood on the trap. Under the caps both were heard to whisper a prayer that was suddenly interrupted. Rev. Bacon stood with his hand raised, looking into the distance. A voice in the crowd had called out. Mathis heard it and turned a second.

"All ready," said Sheriff Harkins in a low voice. The condemned men stood stiff and erect. The keen-edged hatchet cut the rope, and the trap fell with a creaking sound. A sickening hiss was emitted from two throats, followed by two quick snaps, and the bodies dangled at the ends of seven-foot drops.

"Kill that nigger three or four times!" shouted a member of the crowd. "Hang him by the heels!"

The trap fell exactly at 12:50. The crowd that had been so noisy suddenly hushed. No sound penetrated the clear globe of stillness. Both bodies twitched and quivered. Lester was badly affected with the rigors, and his contortions at several junctures were quite violent. Mathis gave one final shudder and went still.

Doctors J. T. Chandler and J. P. Wilkins stood beneath the scaffold with watches in their hands, feeling the pulse of the dying men. This was a first for both physicians: Chandler was only twenty-one years of age and Wilkins only twenty-eight. Chandler would live to see the beginning of the First World War, but Wilkins would die just a year after the events at the scaffold.

The crowd surged to and fro, and several times the deputies were compelled to beat back people who pushed forward to get a closer view of the gruesome end. An observer commented afterward, "The analysis of torture is harrowing. The quiver of the death struggle is beyond analysis. Seven thousand people watched the condemned as if they were dying reptiles. Four women pressed close to the rope and directly in front of the swinging, trembling, tortured men, and viewed the scene with placid interest." Only one report would state that the two necks were broken in the fall. Most generally agreed that they suffocated.

At 1:04, or fourteen minutes after the drop, Mathis was pronounced dead. A half minute later the same verdict was pronounced for Lester.

The bodies were cut down, placed in the coffins, and turned over to the relatives who appeared after the tragic event had ended. The photograph of Mathis' coffin shows that the boxes were merely plain boards that had not been painted or decorated in any way. They had been prepared by W. T. Wallace, the local undertaker.

Will Mathis' coffin after the hanging

None of the relatives of either man had witnessed the execution. According to some later accounts, Mathis' body was claimed by his brothers, Sam and Walker, who had come up from Chickasaw County for the occasion. They took the body east of Oxford to Kingdom Cemetery and buried it there, within two miles of the murder scene. In another version, the body was turned over to Louis Harris, a second cousin to Will Mathis. Harris had brought his wagon to town to bring the body back to Mathis' widow.

Years later, a relative of Will Mathis would recall details of the latter's final trip to Kingdom Cemetery:

> As soon as permission was granted and the body could be released, Louis Harris and Bob Leeton loaded the coffin onto Harris' wagon and began the slow journey out of Oxford back

to Yocona. The weather was getting bad as they rattled along the first eight miles. When they reached Bob Leeton's house, the family was still up but the lamps had been lighted because it was dark. Harris decided to stay there for the night.

Neighborhood friends came with coffee and food, and they sat up with the Leeton family with the coffin inside until daybreak.

The next morning, as soon as the sun was up and the wagon was reloaded, Harris and Leeton rode on the remaining three miles to Kingdom Cemetery. There an open grave awaited. Two small graves were close by. In one rested the body of Marshall, Whit Owens' only son, who had been born March 8, 1899, and died on February 4 the next year. The other grave was that of Daniel, the first child of Will and Cordie Mathis, who was born on February 7, 1901, and lived until March 20 of that year.

Many people, young and old, from the area congregated around the dark pit. Among them, no doubt, were folks who were firmly convinced that Mathis had been wrongfully treated, even "crucified." Yet other people in the group had feared him when he was alive, and they came perhaps to confirm with their own eyes that the terror of their neighborhood had truly been sent to hell.

The burial was a simple one, the casket remaining closed. Mother and son both attended. Cordie was visibly exhausted from being up all night, having returned from Oxford in a buggy with the preacher. At one point in his funeral oration, the preacher is remembered to have said, "This poor woman needs a friend and a home. She does not have one friend and no place to live." Sometime later Cordie sold Will's rifle and other things to pay for the marker that stands over his grave to this day, the words still legible though beginning to be worn away.

The body of Orlando Lester was turned over to his mother, then carried east of town, past the Yocona community, to Cornish Church Cemetery and buried that day.

George Buchanan, the marshal for the Department of Justice in the Northern District of Mississippi, immediately

Mathis' sandstone marker

telegraphed the attorney general: "Mathis & Lester Executed at one o'clock."

The town was orderly throughout the day, in spite of the large assembly, and shortly after the execution the people began wending their way homeward. The details as arranged by Sheriff Harkins and his deputies were perfect in every respect. The entire process had been executed "without a barble," as the *Globe* reported.

Author's Note: While we're considering the last hours, an observation is in order. Folks long after the fact inherited mixed versions of the proceedings. One version has the two criminals riding in the same wagon, sitting on their coffins, accompanied by Rev. Armistead Williams and Rev. W. P. Bacon. At the gallows, one story has it that Cordie was there and made an impassioned plea for mercy. All newspaper accounts have her remain at the jail.

Chapter Seventeen
Justice for Whit Owens

Life is a continuum of events that flows seamlessly and meaninglessly from one to another. Acts end and scenes start with new players coming onto the stage, ignorant of what has preceded. Thus it was in that rainy September of the year 1902 when a new family moved from Ripley, northeast of Oxford, to the university town. In his biography of William Faulkner, Joseph Blotner recalled the words of one of the Falkners upon their arrival:

> "We arrived at Oxford after dark," Jack Falkner recalled later. Sallie Murry and J. W. T. Falkner embraced Maud Falkner and her three little boys as the servants picked up the luggage they had carried with them on their two-day railroad trip. They were hot and cinder-stained from the journey they had made on three separate railroads while Murry was hauling their other possessions overland by wagon. Now they had reached their new home, in the center of north central Mississippi, Jack was stunned.
> We descended from the coach, and Bill and I were speechless with wonder; never had we seen so many people, so many houses and carriages, and so much movement everywhere. And the lights—arc lights! The first we had ever seen. As we drove to Grandfather's house by way of the town square we noticed the fine board sidewalks which extended the whole way. More than that, people were walking along them and it was already past nine o'clock at night. We could hardly wait to see these wonderful sights by daylight.

It was September 24, the first birthday of John Wesley Thompson Falkner III, William's younger brother. The Falkner boys did not know what sort of sight they had missed in not arriving by daylight, nor could they have known that the city was still crowded with those who had not missed it.

So did the author who would write so vividly and painfully about the way Southern whites treated Southern blacks step onto the Oxford stage as a boy. As he and his brothers explored their new hometown the next morning, they were amazed at the number of people, the profusion of stores. After all, with its 1,825 residents Oxford was three times the size of their former town, and people actually referred to Oxford as a city.

The cast overshadowed by the earlier drama were moving on in their lives. Cordie Mathis and her son Clelon were at her mother's house out in the county. Her father, Whit, would shortly be brought back by train from Holly Springs to await the Supreme Court's ruling on his latest appeals. Years later, Cordie would marry DeWitt "D. C." Weeks and bear him one son. In the end she, too, would be laid to rest in Kingdom Cemetery, a stone's throw from the murder site, surrounded by her children and both husbands.

Having been sentenced for two years as an accessory after the fact in the Montgomery murders, George Jackson had already begun his hard labor in the penitentiary, as had his brother, Bill Jackson, under the weight of a life sentence.

In October, petitions to the governor from William Jackson began to appear in the newspapers:

> Petition for Pardon.
> To A. G. Longino, Governor:—
> The undersigned, William Jackson, respectfully petitions you to grant him a pardon, and as reason therefor, states the following:
> He was convicted, at the special term of the Circuit Court of Lafayette County, held in January 1902, of murder on a joint indictment of himself, Whit Owens, Will Mathis and Orlando Lester, for the killing of John A. and Hugh Montgomery, and was sentenced to imprisonment for life in the State Penitentiary, for said alleged crime.

The Mathis family long after the hanging. Clelon is the fellow clasping his hands. The framed image is of Will Mathis.

He is innocent of that crime, and would not have been convicted, but for the fact that he unfortunately happened to be at the scene of the tragedy, only a short time before it occurred, and that fact, coupled with the testimony of Orlando Lester, was, under the high state of feeling then existing, seized upon and relied on, as evidence of guilt.

On his trial, Will Mathis and Mrs. Cordie Mathis both testified that petitioner, while there a short time before the killing, had left and was not there when the killing took place, and had nothing whatever to do with it.

Orlando Lester testified against him, but, as he was being carried back to jail after his testimony against petitioner, told the two deputy sheriffs who had him in charge, that he had sworn falsely against petitioner, and had done so only in the hope of clearing himself; that [Jackson] was not present and did not have anything to do with the killing. With that exception, every eye-witness (including Orlando Lester) to the killing of the Montgomerys, have said repeatedly, and invariably, whether speaking orally to private persons, or by sworn written statements, or when testifying in open court on their various trials, that petitioner is innocent. These statements have been followed up and confirmed in a way that no fair-minded person can doubt their truth, by the fact that on September 24th, 1902, when Will Mathis and Orlando Lester were in the course of being hanged for said crime, and while on the gallows, with noose about their necks, and but a few moments before their souls were ushered into the presence of "Almighty God," said in their dying declaration, "Bill Jackson is innocent."

That, since petitioner's imprisonment, his wife has become insane, as he believes because of his wrongful conviction and punishment, and is now an inmate of the State Lunatic Asylum.

That they have two very young children, one of which was born only a few weeks before his mother lost her mind, and they are being cared for by their aged grandmother, who is without means or physical strength and unable to properly care for them.

Is not that which I have already suffered in being wrongfully convicted of this murder, with eight months imprisonment for a crime I never committed, and the distress consequent to the awful visitation upon my wife, and the helpless condition of my children, sufficient punishment for me, even in the eyes of those who think I ought to be punished for keeping bad company?

Wm. Jackson.

Both William and George Jackson were released from the penitentiary by the fall of 1903. Back in September, weeks before the executions, the *Daily Clarion-Ledger* in Jackson had noted that efforts were already under way to secure a pardon. "An effort will be made, according to advices just received, to secure a pardon for William Jackson, who is now serving a life sentence for complicity in the murder." According to that paper:

> Jackson is exonerated by the confession of Mathis, in which little reliance is placed, but other evidence has been adduced

to show that he did not actually participate in the slaughter of the Montgomery brothers, and only happened to be at the house of Mathis when the deed was committed. Jackson is a criminal of undoubted guilt, and has been indicted for counterfeiting and making moonshine whiskey, but many citizens feel that he should not suffer punishment for a crime of which he is not guilty, and if he is released it is believed that it will have some effect in restoring the reason of his wife, who has been confined in the insane hospital ever since the horrible tragedy.

The dying words of Mathis and Lester had finally moved the state to release Jackson from his life sentence. His freedom was restored, but as one of Whit Owens' defense attorneys later stated before the Mississippi Supreme Court, "It is impossible to restore William Jackson's wife to health."

The *Oxford Eagle* printed and sold "The Life of Will Mathis" for twenty-five cents apiece, collecting many quarters in the process. The set of seven ruled notebooks in which Lester had written his story, however, were never published.

A few days after the executions, the scaffold was dismantled so that the wood could be used elsewhere. The *Oxford Eagle* noted in passing that the rope that had been around Will Mathis' neck had been stolen from the sheriff's office.

The December 28, 1902, issue of the *Globe* had carried its usual potpourri of interesting happenings around town, beginning with:

> Merry Christmas to you. The planned new fire house was claimed as another sign of progress. It was regrettable that the mail trains had been cut off the previous Sunday and Monday. Folks looking for a bargain need only visit the store of M. E. Keys to find Xmas and colored candles and fireworks. Mr. Thomas, of Batesville, was a visitor to the city the day before. And Mr. Bob Hill, of College Hill, was in town last Saturday. And, by the way, have you seen those beautiful doll beds at Buffaloes? Mr. Charlie Gates visited with friends in Memphis on Sunday. Santa Claus is in town and stopping at Buffaloes.

Frank Foust has been engaged for another year as manager of the water and sewerage systems.

And Whit Owens is again a star boarder at the county jail.

He was the final member of the moonshine gang whose fate had not yet been decided. Owens' lawyers had appealed on two separate convictions, and he was spending his days in the Lafayette County lockup. In March 1903, the State Supreme Court would reverse and remand the hanging verdict for the murder of Hugh Montgomery (which had been issued in January 1902), sending it back to Lafayette County for disposition.

As for his life sentence determined after his early September trial in Holly Springs for the Montgomery murders, confusion existed as to what the jury intended by its verdict. They clearly found Owens guilty but were not in agreement about the punishment he should receive. They had been instructed to find him guilty or not guilty, and if guilty he was to be executed or sent to the penitentiary for life. The high court ruled that when the jury had been polled, they clearly did not agree on the term of imprisonment and hence had not rendered a legal verdict upon which the judge could pass sentence.

A recap of Owens' legal proceedings is needed, since he had so many trials. He had been tried for the murder of Hamp Williams at the regular term of the circuit court in Oxford on September 11, 1902, almost two weeks before the executions. His request for a change of venue for this trial had been denied by Judge Lowrey, although the case involved the same witnesses and the circumstances were inextricably woven together with the Montgomery case. When that Williams trial began, only a week had passed since his trial for the murder of John A. Montgomery at Holly Springs, the one where the jury couldn't make up its mind. It may have seemed to Whit Owens that the State was relentlessly hounding him, persecuting rather than prosecuting him. The jury found him guilty of the murder of Hamp Williams and the wounding of Walter Jones, and he was sentenced to hang. Again his defense attorneys, Senator H. V. Sullivan and H. D. Stephens, appealed the sentence to the Mississippi Supreme Court.

In its finding, the Supreme Court held that this constituted reversible error, noting that, although the Williams murder had stirred up little excitement when it happened, the subsequent slayings of the Montgomerys and the fact that so many persons were part of both stories, a linkage existed. Therefore, if a change of venue had been justified in earlier cases, a change of venue should have been awarded in the September Williams case.

"Reversed and remanded," they declared.

Judge Lowrey granted the change of venue on March 19, 1903, thus moving Owens' trial for the Williams murder to Water Valley, fifteen miles to the south in Yalobusha County. At that point, Owens was to face two judges and two juries in almost simultaneous trials: one in Holly Springs concerning the Montgomery killing, the other in Water Valley concerning Hamp Williams. It was indeed fortunate that the railroad connected these two little towns, with Oxford between them, providing relative ease in transporting defendant, trial officials, and witnesses to the two trials.

The Holly Springs trial began in the first week in September 1903 and did not take long. Without Mathis and Lester able to testify, the trial concluded with an acquittal for the accused.

The trial in Water Valley also was relatively brief, and only a few new wrinkles would be introduced. Because Will Mathis was not present, US Attorney M. A. Montgomery was asked by District Attorney Brewer from Yalobusha County to recall what had been said at the first trial. Over the objections of Owens' defense counsel, Montgomery recalled one telling conversation he'd had with Mathis:

A. [H]e had suggested at one time killing him by poisoning, by putting poison in a water-melon, and that he, Will Mathis said to him, "If you had put the poison in that watermelon," I believe he said, he himself would have been killed instead of the negro Hamp Williams, [or] along with the negro Hamp Williams. He said also that he told this negro to go to the church and select a place there and kill him at the church.

By the Court: Who told him that?

A. Whit Owens sent the negro Orlando to this church the evening of the killing to kill him there. Now that's the conversation that Will Mathis stated that he had with the Defendant, Whit Owens. He said that they had been talking about this killing for some time, probably a month before the killing took place, and finally determined upon this plan, that is about all now that I recollect without being called especially to it.

Q. I will ask you Professor, if he said anything, if you remember, he said anything with regard to whether or not he and Owens had been connected in the distilling business, illicit stilling business?

Sullivan: Defendant objects; that is not a question.

Court overruled and the Defendant then and there excepted.

A. He said that they had been engaged in that business, he and Whit Owens for about four years, that he had, that he began making whiskey on Whit Owens' still; and that he was afterwards asked if he had a still of his own, and he said he had, that his still at this particular time had been captured by officers back in the month of August. He said also that Whit Owens had a still at this time, the time of the killing in Knight's field, there near Owens' house.

Q. Was that his testimony in this case?

A. That's my recollection.

Q. I will ask you what, if he said anything, with reference to where Orlando lived?

A. I couldn't say whether I have any recollection about what, where Will Mathis said he lived. I have no recollection in this particular case, if you will let me refer to this, I can answer that, he was living at that time with Whit Owens and had been for some time; I thought you were referring though to the place he lived, how far from Whit Owens.

Q. I will ask you what Mathis said, if anything, in the

testimony on the trial of this case, as to who they were trying to kill at the time they killed Hamp Williams.

A. He said it was the intention Whit Owens said to kill these witnesses, Walter Jones, Alfred Neering, two witnesses, were witnesses against Orlando Lester.

The judgment at stake in this trial was whether punishment should be set at life imprisonment or hanging. The secondhand testimony may have had an effect on the leniency of Owens' sentencing, for, as the *Oxford Globe* reported, "Water Valley, Miss., Nov. 3—(Special) —The jury in the case of the State vs. Whit Owens charged with the killing of Hamp Williams returned a verdict of guilty this morning at half past ten o'clock. A motion for a new trial was overruled by the court and the defendant was sentenced to the penitentiary for life."

Because of the condition of the Yalobusha County jail, the judge ordered that Owens be held in the Lafayette County jail until his transportation to Jackson. Owens had been incarcerated continuously since the Montgomery murders back in November 1901. His lawyers immediately filed their fourth petition on his behalf to the State Supreme Court. All of this took a great deal of time, and in the meantime Owens remained in the county jail in Oxford.

Finally, on April 9, 1904, the judges at the high court in Jackson handed down their opinion: "Affirmed."

One of the defense attorneys, H. D. Stephens, submitted a Brief for the Appellant in which he pointed out a large number of legal errors attributed to the prosecution and lower court. Owens' other attorney, Senator H. V. Sullivan, also submitted a brief. He portrayed Owens as "a peaceable and law abiding man—that loved and took care of one wife, and five little girls—who the record shows—was a good neighbor. It is a sad fact that he had a bad son in law, Will Mathis, whom he could not control, and whom he declined to support in the dirty work of double murder. One can and should be responsible for their associates, but not their kin, the one relation is voluntary, the other is not."

The good senator might have sensed a predisposition on the side of the justices, because he was moved to ask during his presentation, "Is the Court tired of the Whit Owens case as has been said? And therefore an affirmance? The very suggestion is unworthy of repetition—except to contrast it with the higher estimate that everyone places on the Bench of Mississippi." Their verdict gives much credence to his perception that they were tired after hearing three other appeals from Owens. In an unpublished finding, the Court affirmed the Water Valley lower court sentence: "Guilty, with life in the penitentiary."

Supreme Court minutes dated May 9, 1904, offer this information:

> Without reference to the action of the court in regard to the copy of the stenographer's notes, and without reference to the manner of using said copy of said notes by some of the witnesses in delivering their testimony, we think the verdict well warranted by the other competent testimony in the case.
> Affirmed.
> Whitfield, C. J.

There was no further recourse for an appeal. Owens was returned to the Lafayette County Jail to await his transfer to the state penitentiary to begin the rest of his life. His prison file contains the following observations about prisoner number 238: He was fifty years old when he entered on May 24, 1904, he was 5'6," weighed 140 pounds, complexion light, hair light, eyes blue, build heavy, face round, nose large and sharp, scar on left shoulder blade caused by boil, one long scar on inside left big toe, one round scar on front part of ankle of right foot. He was a farmer. He was incarcerated for murder.

If Owens had to go to prison, he went at an almost fortuitous moment. Hardly a decade earlier the penal system had relied on the chain gang approach to punishment. Around this time major reform had been put in place to rid the system of corruption. The state penitentiary came to be known as the prison without walls. Instead of one facility in which all convicts were incarcerated, there now were established farms in several locations where inmates could do agricultural work, manufacture goods, and generally provide income to support the system. The whole operation became nearly self-sustaining.

One other note is worth mentioning: the system was entirely segregated by race, and all white prisoners were sent to the Rankin County Prison Farm near Jackson, the state capital. Also, the system provided longtimers with good records the possibility of being made trustees, giving them the responsibility of guarding others and affording them a few extra benefits.

Whit Owens was evidently a model prisoner, because he became a trustee very quickly. One of the rewards of his position was that he had a separate house of his own at the prison farm and his wife could visit him there. The following entry is listed in the Minutes of the Trustees of the Mississippi Penitentiary for November 1, 1910:

> Ordered that a former order restricting visits of convicts' families to every six months be amended as follows: "That the immediate family of a convict shall be allowed to visit once every 30 days, but only between the hours of 8 AM and 6 PM. All other relatives and friends may visit only once every six months, said visit to be made between above stated hours."

The last entry in Owens' penitentiary record indicates that he was released on January 13, 1912, after serving only seven and a half years of his life sentence, ten years if the time spent in county jails during the various trials is added. This final record entry concludes with why he was released early: "Discharged for meritorious conduct displayed by him in preventing a fellow convict from escaping. On recommendation of Superintendent and Board of Trustees."

Whit and Martha Owens after he was released from prison

Although the State of Mississippi had no parole provisions, there was a "good time law" and a provision for trustees to be discharged when they were instrumental in preventing fellow convicts from escaping. Whit Owens finally went home and lived another sixteen years.

Life in Oxford, Mississippi, would go on as before. The memories of the exploits of a country moonshining gang would dim as the years passed. Local tales of a new sort, told by a resident who would become arguably the greatest American writer of all time, would stir younger generations. The oppression of a race because of the darkness of their skin would continue throughout the century to come. Yet with the passing of time, the Deep South would gradually change, become tamed like all of the other parts of the United States. The saga of two moonshiners, Will Mathis and Orlando Lester, now stands forever as a legacy of a high-spirited, reckless era that will never return.

Bibliography

Joseph Blotner. *Faulkner: A Biography*, Random House, 1974.

Marvel Ramey Sisk, "Crime Drama in Oxford, Mississippi," 1971.

Jackson Daily Clarion-Ledger, 1901-1902.

Memphis Commercial Appeal, 1901-1902.

New Orleans Picayune, 1901-1902.

Oxford Eagle, 1901-1902.

Oxford Globe, 1901-1902.

David McElreath, Chester Quarles, John Ramey, "The Last Public Hanging in Oxford," American Jails, Vol. 20, 2006.

"The Life of Will Mathis," Will Mathis, 1902.

Index

Adams, R. S., 51
African Americans, 36-37, 39-45, 52-53, 62, 66, 72, 76, 84-85, 92, 100, 106, 108, 127, 140, 142, 148, 152-54, 175-76, 178, 188, 192, 196, 201-2, 209-10, 219, 227, 231, 234, 248
Anderson, Gene, 34

Bacon, N. W. P., 117, 228, 231-32, 234-35
Bramlett, A. C., 173, 194-96, 199
Buchanan, George M., 97, 103, 114, 121, 138, 238

Chandler, J. T., 236
Commercial Appeal, 25, 44, 103, 105, 107, 115, 117, 120-21, 130, 139, 175, 207, 213, 218, 221, 234
Cullen, Linburn, 184, 188

Dallas, Mississippi, 59, 101, 108, 109, 115, 220
Davis, Reuben, 133
Delay, Mississippi, 24-25, 32, 48, 58-59, 95, 102, 119-20
Denmark post office, 110
Dennis, George, 52, 210
Denton, Tom, 42
Dickey, H. C., 139
Dogtown, Mississippi, 91
dog trackers, 103
Du Bois, W. E. B., 41

Fuller, J. T., 200

Hall, Curdie, 90, 209
Harkins, John, 58, 96, 116-17, 121, 128, 177, 183-84, 186, 189, 195, 212, 215, 224, 228-29, 231, 234-35, 239
Harkins, Tom, 95-96, 202-3
Harris, Louis, 237
Hartfield, Curt, 108
Holly Springs, Mississippi, 247
Holmes, J. E., 114, 135, 169, 190
Hyde, B. L., 125

Ivy, W. F., 173, 199

Jackson, Bill, 61, 67, 72-74, 77-78, 84, 86, 90-92, 94, 101-2, 119, 126, 131-32, 134-35, 146, 148-49, 156, 158, 161, 166, 169-72, 175, 187, 191, 200, 204, 206, 227-28, 233-34, 242, 244
Jackson, George, 76, 89-91, 101, 104, 106-7, 131, 148, 175, 228, 244
Jones, Walter, 50, 52-55, 92, 210

Kimbrough, D. M., 132, 138, 148
Kimmons, J. H., 135, 169
Kingdom Cemetery, 28, 237-38, 242
Leeton, Bob, 237-38
Lester, Orlando, 21-22, 36-37, 39, 42, 46-47, 50, 52-54, 61, 63, 65-66, 68-69, 72-74, 76-77, 79, 81-82, 85-87, 89, 94, 101, 106, 126, 130-33, 141-42, 146, 148, 151-52, 160, 164-66, 168, 170-72,

176-78, 182, 186, 189, 190-92, 194-95, 200, 203-7, 209, 211-14, 217-18, 220, 223, 228, 233, 235-36, 238-39, 242-45, 247, 249, 252
Longino, Andrew Houston, 186, 205, 213, 220, 242
Lowrey, Perrin H., 117, 119, 121, 132-33, 135, 163, 171, 173, 175, 183, 185-87, 189-90, 213, 246-47
lynching, 39, 44-45, 111, 116, 121, 128, 163, 174, 179, 182, 185

Markette, Ben, 184
Mask, George, 28, 36, 53-54, 66, 83, 141-42, 145, 157, 165, 168, 191, 203, 212
Mathis, Baxter Cleveland "Clelon," 28, 136, 242
Mathis, Cordie, 28, 61-62, 65, 75, 80, 94, 101, 106, 110, 117, 127, 131, 133, 136, 153, 160, 170, 200, 219, 221, 228, 233, 238, 242-43
Mathis, Eliza, 137
Mathis, Sam (Will's brother), 210, 237
Mathis, Samuel (Will's father), 137
Mathis, Walker, 210, 237
Mathis, Will, 21-22, 24-26, 28, 31, 33-39, 46-55, 59-92, 94-97, 99-111, 114-17, 119-20, 123, 125-45, 147-53, 155-58, 160, 162-66, 169, 170-73, 175-78, 181-82, 186-87, 190-95, 199-207, 209-24, 226-39, 242-45, 247-49, 252
Matthews, Doak, 229
Matthews, Frank, 59, 138, 170
Matthews, J. F., 97
Matthews, P. E., 166
Mills (Presbyterian reverend), 162
Mississippi State Penitentiary, 78, 172

mobs, 21, 45, 100, 108, 110, 116-17, 127, 131, 135, 179-80, 183-84, 193, 225, 230
Montgomery, Dave, 167, 199
Montgomery, Hugh, 22, 50-51, 55, 59, 61-64, 67, 69, 75-77, 84-86, 89-90, 92-94, 101, 119, 124-26, 131, 134, 138-39, 148, 151-53, 167, 170-72, 175, 186, 194, 197-98, 203-4, 207, 213, 219, 234, 242, 246
Montgomery, John A., 22, 55, 59, 60-63, 67, 69, 75, 77, 85, 89, 92-93, 101, 107, 122-23, 125-26, 131, 133-34, 139, 148-49, 152, 165, 170, 172, 181, 189, 198, 213, 219, 234, 242
Montgomery, M. A., 54, 116, 131, 138, 163, 173, 189-90, 212, 224, 228, 247
moonshine, 31, 47, 51, 72, 77, 97, 99, 147, 164, 174, 206, 225, 228, 245-46
Murphy, "Scoon," 188
Murray, Bobby, 104

New Orleans Picayune, 64, 136, 150
Niles, Henry Clay, 121, 131

Oliver, Dick, 116
Owens, Brice, 227
Owens, Charley, 227
Owens, Martha, 27-28, 31, 82, 242
Owens, Whit, 22, 25, 27-28, 31-32, 34-38, 51, 53-54, 65-66, 68, 72, 77, 81-87, 89, 92-94, 100-101, 106, 108, 123, 127, 131-34, 136, 140-43, 145-47, 150, 152, 154-55, 159-60, 164-69, 171-74, 176-78, 182-200, 202-17, 220, 225-28, 232-33, 238, 241-42, 245-52
Oxford Eagle, 25, 40, 49, 58, 105, 119, 163, 171, 178, 187, 245
Oxford Globe, 25, 39, 41-42, 86-87,

120, 125, 213, 219, 249

Parchman, Mississippi, 175, 183-85
Pilcher, Hiram, 49
Pilcher, Jim, 64
Pontotoc Sentinel, 124, 186
Porter, R. G., 117, 125, 228
posses, 43-44, 46, 96-97, 101, 103-08, 115, 230

Ragland, Tom, 100, 105-6, 116, 162, 167, 195, 198, 215, 217, 224, 229, 231, 235
Ramey, Hal, 175
Ramey, Pete, 48, 58, 96, 109, 116-17, 128, 184, 225, 229-31
Roane, W. A., 63, 77-79, 89, 93-94, 116, 124, 127, 138, 140-42, 149-53, 156-57, 159-61, 163, 169, 186, 189-90, 205, 207, 213
Roebuck, Lonnie, 92, 96
Rogers, Dave, 36, 48, 102, 132, 235
Rowland, P. W., 87, 123, 149

Sanders, Will, 43
Sisk, Marvel Ramey, 58, 96, 99, 106, 116, 183
Sivley, C. L., 138, 169, 189-90
Slough, C. E., 94, 132, 135, 178, 197, 200, 211
Somerville, T. H., 178
Springdale Church, 49
Standifer, Jennifer, 64, 136, 143, 145, 150
Stephens, H. D., 190, 247, 249
Stephens, Z. M., 47, 132, 169, 188-89, 191, 203, 208
Steward, John, 106
Stone, James, 138
Sullivan, H. V., 247, 249

Temple, E. E., 229
Thompson, Henry, 95, 142, 202
Toccopola, Mississippi, 108

Vines, Ken, 90-91
Vines, Shell, 154, 202

Washington, Booker Taliaferro, 41
Water Valley, Mississippi, 177, 183, 203, 211, 247, 249-50
Water Valley, Tennessee, 103-5
Weeks, DeWitt Clinton "D. C.," 28, 242
Welch, Dan, 28, 59, 88, 91, 93, 96, 170, 197, 199-200
Welch, Ellen, 78-79, 92, 140-41, 191
Welch, John, 48-49
Wilkins, J. P., 236
Williams, A. W., 229, 231, 235
Williams, Hamp, 51-55, 65, 92, 140, 189-90, 201, 204-5, 207, 209, 211-12, 214, 216, 246-49
Wilson, J. C., 138, 169
Winter, A. M., 43
Woods, George, 52

Yocona, Mississippi, 59, 230, 238
Yocona River, 59, 91, 99, 102, 106, 108
Young, A. A., 123, 150, 197-98